Excerpts from
Bands 1 and 9, Side A, of
MELODII TUVY (GOST 5289-73,
33D–030773): "Reka Alash," sung by Oorzhak
Khunashtaar-ool in the "sigit" or "whistling" style;

PLACE COIN HERE IF
SOUNDSHEET SLIPS
33 1/3 RPM
MONAURAL

"Artyy Saiyr," sung by D. Damba-Darzha in the
"kargyraa" or "wheezing" style, accompanied
by A. Laptan on the byzaanchi. Reproduced
with permission from Melodiya
Records, Moscow USSR.

MFD. IN U.S.A. BY
107304-1A
EVATONE® CLEARWATER, FL.
SOUNDSHEETS

TUVA OR BUST!

TUVA OR BUST!

RICHARD FEYNMAN'S
LAST JOURNEY

Ralph Leighton

W·W·Norton & Company

New York   London

Book jacket: collage of Tuva memorabilia assembled by the author;
photograph of Richard Feynman (pushing automobile), Glen Cowan,
and Ralph Leighton courtesy Tohru Ohnuki.
Stamps courtesy of George Alevezos.

Printed in the United States of America.

The text of this book is composed

in 11/13.5 Goudy Old Style,

with the display set

in ITC Garamond Bold and Goudy Old Style.

Composition and manufacturing by

The Haddon Craftsmen, Inc.

Book design by Margaret M. Wagner.

First Edition

Library of Congress Cataloging-in-Publication Data

Leighton, Ralph.

Tuva or bust! : Richard Feynman's last journey/

by Ralph Leighton.

p.   cm.

Includes index.

1. Feynman, Richard Phillips—Journeys—Central
Asia—Tuvinskaia A.S.S.R. 2. Tuvinskaia A.S.S.R. (Russian
S.F.S.R.)—Description and travel. 3. Physicists—United
States—Biography.

I. Title.

QC16.F49L45 1991

957.5—dc20 90–42206

ISBN 0–393–02953–0

W.W. Norton & Company, Inc.

500 Fifth Avenue, New York, N.Y. 10110

W.W. Norton & Company, Ltd.

10 Coptic Street, London WC1A 1PU

1 2 3 4 5 6 7 8 9 0

Contents

To the Reader   7

1. There Is No Such Country   13
2. Forty-five Snowy I   18
3. Mysterious Melodies   39
4. Hail to the Chief!   62
5. We Appear in the Center of Asia   74
6. Three Americans Reach Tuva   90
7. Meeting in Moscow   104
8. Amateur Ambassadors   130
9. Clowns or Con Men?   148
10. The Keller Accord   168
11. The Trip Is Arranged   185
12. Catalina Cowboys   203

13. The Invitation Arrives   2 1 4

14. Epilogue   2 2 1

    Appendix A: Protocol   2 3 1

    Appendix B: WELCOME BY RICHARD
    FEYNMAN   2 4 1

    Appendix C: FRIENDS OF TUVA   2 4 5

    Index   2 4 7

    PAINTING OF RICHARD FEYNMAN   2 5 6

To the Reader

RICHARD P. FEYNMAN (1918–1988) was an
illustrious professor of physics at the California
Institute of Technology (Caltech) from the early
1950s through the late 1980s. Upon graduation
from Princeton he was recruited to work on the
Manhattan Project at Los Alamos. To entertain
himself he perfected his safecracking abilities—
at one point opening the combination locks behind which lay all the secrets to the atomic
bomb—and left notes scrawled in red pointing
out the laxity of security in the government's
most secret project.[1]

Near the end of his life he was again recruited
by the government, this time to serve on the
Rogers Commission investigating the space
shuttle *Challenger* disaster. Again, Feynman

[1]These exploits and others are described in *Surely You're Joking,
Mr. Feynman!*, published by W. W. Norton in 1985 and by Bantam
in 1989. See also Footnote 4 on the following page.

entertained himself in a way that sent shock waves through the establishment: at a public hearing he squeezed a piece of rubber "O-ring" with a C-clamp and dipped them into a glass of ice water. His "little experiment" to show the rubber's lack of resilience at cold temperatures stripped away NASA's attempts at obfuscation and revealed the primary cause of the accident.[2]

Because he was a colleague of my father, who edited *The Feynman Lectures on Physics*,[3] Feynman occasionally visited our home. One time, when I was in high school, my musician friend Thomas Rutishauser happened to be over. Having heard that Feynman was an accomplished drummer, we asked him to join us.

"I didn't bring my drums," he said.

"That's okay," I said. "You can use one of these small tables here."

Intrigued by their sound, and perhaps also attracted to the rhythms Tom and I were playing, the professor grabbed a small table for himself and joined in. Thus began some of the happiest times of my life: the three of us would meet every week for a session of drumming—on tables, bongos, and congas—interspersed with breaks during which Feynman would recount one of his amazing adventures.[4]

A dozen years ago I fell into one of those adventures myself. While I was not accompanied at every turn by the "curious character" (as Feynman liked to describe himself), I gradually became infected with his zest for life on every

[2]Feynman's experiences in Washington are recounted in *What Do You Care What Other People Think?*, published by W. W. Norton in 1988 and by Bantam in 1989.
[3]Published by Addison-Wesley in 1964 and reissued in 1989.
[4]A cassette and CD re-creating one of those soirées of drumming and storytelling were produced as a charity project by the author and radio engineer Tohru Ohnuki. Copies of *Safecracker Suite* can be obtained by sending $10 for an audiocassette, or $15 for a CD, payable to: Ralph Leighton, Box 70021, Pasadena, CA 91117 USA. All proceeds benefit the John Wayne Cancer Clinic at UCLA.

level—especially his passion for the unexpected. As it turned out, most of what happened on our quest got us no closer to our goal. But had we not embarked on the journey, we would have missed it all.

Feynman compared his adventures to fishing: one must wait patiently for long periods of time before something interesting happens. I never heard of Feynman actually going fishing. Had he gone out on a lake with a fishing pole, I'm sure he would affirm what many anglers already know: you will be disappointed only if you decide beforehand that you're going fishing in order to catch a fish.

As with life, I think this story will be enjoyed most if the reader does not decide beforehand what it is about.

Pasadena, California
Shagaa, 1991

TUVA OR BUST!

There Is No Such Country

THE plates were being cleared from the table, and I had just begun finishing off the salad— part of what had become a weekly ritual at the Feynmans'. Richard, always at the north end of the grand table, traded witticisms with son Carl, who shared the lengthy east side of the table with the guest. To the south sat Gweneth, making sure the food moved smoothly around the table, and daughter Michelle occupied the west.

It was late in the summer of 1977. Michelle was about to enter the second grade at a local elementary school; Carl was ready to begin his junior year at the high school in Pasadena where I would be teaching mathematics and coaching water polo.

"Math is okay," I said, "but what I really like is geography. If I had a geography class I would bring in my shortwave radio and tune in the BBC or Radio Nederland. We'd play geography games like I did with my brother: he and I would

1

go through every independent country of the world. You know, the last letter of Liechtenstein determines the first letter of the next country—Nepal, for example."

"Or Nigeria, Niger, or Nicaragua," said Carl, with a hint of his mother's Yorkshire accent.

"And after exhausting the independent countries," I continued, "we would move on to provinces. Did you know there's a province called 'Amazonas' in three different countries?"

"Let's see," said Carl. "How about Brazil, Colombia, and Peru?"

"Not bad," I replied. "The third country is Venezuela, although Peru does have more of the Amazon in it than Venezuela does."

"So you think you know every country in the world?" interjected Richard in a familiar, mischievous voice that usually signaled impending doom for its target.

"Uh, sure," I said, taking another bite of salad, preparing myself for the embarrassment that was sure to follow.

"Okay, then what ever happened to Tannu Tuva?"

"Tannu what?" I said. "I never heard of it."

"When I was a kid," Richard continued, "I used to collect stamps. There were some wonderful triangular and diamond-shaped stamps that came from a place called 'Tannu Tuva.' "

I became suspicious. My brother Alan, a stamp collector, had made a fool out of me dozens of times when we played "Islands of the World." He would rattle off some exotic-sounding name like "Aitutaki," and when I challenged him on it he would pull out his stamp catalog and show me a few stamps from the place. So I stopped challenging him, and he grew bolder and bolder, winning game after game. Finally I caught him on "Aknaki," supposedly part of a tiny atoll in the South Pacific, after dimly recalling that the week before he had claimed it was a river in Mauritania. So I straightened up in my chair a bit and said, "Sir, there is no such country."

"Sure there is," said Richard. "In the 1930s it was a purple splotch on the map near Outer Mongolia, and I've never heard anything about it ever since."

Had I stopped and thought a moment, I would have realized that Richard's favorite trick was to say something unbelievable that turns out to be true. Instead, I tightened the noose that had just been placed around my neck: "The only countries near Outer Mongolia are China and the Soviet Union," I said, boldly. "I can show you on the map."

I grabbed my last bite of salad as we all got up from the table and proceeded into the living room to Richard's favorite book, the *Encyclopaedia Britannica*. In the last volume there was an atlas. We opened it to a map of Asia.

"See?" I said. "There's nothing here but the USSR, Mongolia, and China. This 'Tannu Tuva' must have been somewhere else."

"Oh, look!" said Carl. "Tuvinskaya ASSR. It's bordered on the south by the Tannu-Ola Mountains."

Sure enough, occupying a notch northwest of Mongolia was a territory that could well once have had the name Tannu Tuva. I thought, I've been had by a stamp collector again!

"Look at this," remarked Richard. "The capital is spelled K-Y-Z-Y-L."

"That's crazy," I said. "There's not a legitimate vowel anywhere!"

"We must go there," said Gweneth.

"Yeah!" exclaimed Richard. "A place that's spelled K-Y-Z-Y-L has just *got* to be interesting!"

Richard and I grinned at each other and shook hands.

Everyone returned to the dining room for tea and dessert. As the conversation continued, I thought of the classic question, "Why are you climbing that mountain?" Our "mountain" had no particular physical challenge to it, but reaching a place controlled by the USSR in the deepest interior of Asia was sure to be difficult. And our reason for undertaking this challenge was downright profound compared to the classic answer: "Because it's spelled K-Y-Z-Y-L!"

We discussed how we might reach our goal. Of course Richard could give a series of physics lectures in Moscow, and we could all go to Kyzyl afterwards. (Actually, anyone traveling under such circumstances should insist on going to Tuva *first*, in case some sort of "difficulty" arose after the lectures.) But reaching Tuva that way would be like riding in a helicopter to the summit.

Richard had journeyed to remote corners of the world before. Gweneth recounted how, a few years before, they had trekked for two weeks on foot with a friend and a Mexican graduate student into a mountainous region of northwest Mexico. They descended into a canyon, the Barranca de Cobre—said to be longer and deeper than the Grand Canyon—and met Tarahumara Indians who had had very little contact with the outside world. Richard had borrowed a Tarahumara-Spanish dictionary from UCLA and learned some phrases from it, but when he spoke to them in their native language, the Indians suspected he was a Mexican government official! After convincing them otherwise, Richard was offered the local intoxicating brew by the Tarahumara as a gesture of honor. (Richard normally did not touch alcohol, but made an exception in this case.) Gweneth and Richard enjoyed the adventure so much that they returned to the region a year later.

After dinner Richard and I continued the weekly ritual, going downstairs to drum in his studio. Although we had been drumming together for ten years by now, that "primitive" activity still had not lost any of its power.

During one of our breaks Richard went over to the bookcase, which was filled to the brim with books, technical papers, exotic rhythm instruments, and artist's sketch pads. Soon he pulled out an old, slim book and opened it. It was an atlas from 1943. And there, on the map of Asia, next to Outer Mongolia, was that purple splotch called Tannu Tuva.

Forty-five Snowy I

2 THE school year washed over me, leaving barely a moment to breathe: a typical day began with coaching the water polo team at 6 A.M., followed by five classes of remedial arithmetic and beginning algebra, and then back to coaching water polo. Most weekends included more coaching, but two welcome exceptions came in November, when Richard and I went to San Francisco to drum for a small ballet company whose home was the Elks Lodge near Union Square.

The year before, we had composed and performed the music for *Cycles of Supersitition,* a ballet by the same company. Our "music" consisted entirely of drumming, which was perfectly adequate as far as Richard was concerned. He regarded conventional music with its chords and melodies as "drumming with notes"—an unnecessary complication.

Cycles of Superstition had been a great success:

the audience of perhaps thirty applauded enthusiastically. This year the production was called *The Ivory Merchant.* Our job was to portray the interaction of colonial and native cultures in Africa, again entirely through drumming.

Rehearsals were Friday evening and Saturday evening, with performances the following weekend. During our free time on Saturday we walked the streets of San Francisco. Our conversation hit upon Tuva. "Let's go over to the San Francisco library," suggested Richard. "It oughta be pretty good."

Half an hour later we reached the Civic Center, a collection of European-style buildings built around a large square lined with those elegantly manicured *marronier* trees found all over France. The library faced the City Hall, where the United Nations convened for the first time, in 1945. As we made our way up the wide stone stairway, Richard proposed a challenge: to find a picture of Tuva in this library.

When we looked through the card catalog, we realized we'd be lucky to find anything at all on Tuva. There was no heading for "Tannu Tuva," "Tuva," or "Tuvinskaya ASSR." There was a section on Central Asia, but it featured places like Tashkent and Samarkand.

Richard went off into the stacks to look at the books on "Siberia—description and travel," while I wandered around the reference section. I eventually hit upon the 1953 edition of the *Great Soviet Encyclopedia* and found an article on Kyzyl. In the middle of the page was a black-and-white photograph—a picture of Tuva!—which showed the "Dom Sovietov," Tuva's new government building. The architecture was not unlike that of the City Hall outside. A lone automobile stood conspicuously in front, casting no shadow—it seemed to have been hand-painted into the photograph.

Excited, I went looking for Richard.

He was still in "Siberia—description and travel," sitting on the floor, reading a book called *Road to Oblivion.* The title looked promising. The author, Vladimir Zenzinov, had been sent into exile by the Czar—not once, not twice, but three times. The first two times he managed to escape, so the third time, the government was determined to put him in a place so isolated he would never find his way out. Even though that place turned out not to be Tuva, Richard was captivated by the story.[1]

The following weekend we performed *The Ivory Merchant* to an audience of about fifteen—hardly enough to account for the relatives and friends of the cast. Depressed at the sight of so many vacant chairs, I said, "This reminds me of eating in an empty restaurant."

"If the food is good, what does it matter?" replied Richard. "Just do your best. Remember what we're doing: we're composing and performing music for a ballet, man!"

It was an unusual thing for a professor of physics and a high school math teacher to be doing, but we were doing it, and Richard loved that. But he abhorred Samuel Johnson's observation about a dog walking on its hind legs—"It is not done well, but you are surprised to find it done at all"—so it was not mentioned in the program that the drummers had other professions.

A month later, at Christmas, the predictable pattern in my family of presenting phonograph records to each other was broken by Alan, who gave me some of the wonderful triangular and diamond-shaped stamps from the 1930s that Richard had talked about. They showed exciting scenes of horsemen at full gallop, kneeling archers taking aim, wrestlers interlocked in struggle, hunters shooting their quarry at close range (after all, they were postage stamps!), and a wide variety of wild and domesticated animals from foxes and sables to

---

[1]Retracing my steps in 1990, more than ten years later, turned out to be daunting: the stacks in the San Francisco library were closed to the public (I had to talk my way in); the upper levels were still in disarray, with nearly all the books toppled to the floor by the earthquake that hit the Bay Area in October 1989.

yaks, camels, and reindeer. Such great variety in so small a country seemed impossible. Were the scenes in these postage stamps based on fact or fantasy? Around the border of several stamps were strange designs—festival masks of some sort— and the words "Poşta Touva," spelled as if the territory had once been ruled by France.

During Christmas vacation I went to the UCLA library and discovered *Unknown Mongolia* (London, 1913) by the English explorer Douglas Carruthers (in which Tuva is referred to as "the basin of the Upper Yenisei" and its inhabitants as "the Uriankhai") and half a dozen other books about Tuva, all of which I borrowed. Apart from *Unknown Mongolia,* all the books were in Russian, a language reputed to be twice as hard as German. But because mathematical formulas contain Greek letters, and the Greek alphabet formed the basis for the Russian alphabet, Richard was able to make out some of the captions. I bought a pocket Russian-English dictionary and looked up words one by one.

One of the UCLA library books showed the first government building—a log cabin—with a beautiful white yurt next to it. There were inevitable jokes about the president of Tuva sleeping in the "White Yurt."

Another book had several pictures of Kyzyl. The new government building was already familiar to us. Other photographs showed the regional Party headquarters, a post office, and a hotel. Because the photographs were taken from different locations and included more than one building, we were able to piece together a crude map of downtown Kyzyl. In none of the photographs did we see more than one automobile.

One picture caught my interest only much later: Shkola No. 2. After deducing that there must be at least two schools in Kyzyl, I realized that here was a definite place in Tuva I could write to: I'm a teacher, so why not write to a teacher in

Tuva and ask how I can visit? As much fun as it was to find out more about Tuva, our real goal was to get to Kyzyl, and so far we hadn't done anything about that.

I contacted Mary Fleming Zirin, a woman I had bummed rides off of when I was a student at UCLA, where she was working on her Ph.D. in Russian. Mary remembered me, and agreed to translate a short letter to "Teacher" at Shkola No. 2 in Kyzyl. For good measure I sent a similar letter to Shkola No. 1, Kyzyl, Tuva, USSR.

In the spring, after the high school swimming season and its coaching responsibilities were over, I went to the library at the University of Southern California and searched through immigration records of 1900–1950 to see if anyone had come from Tuva to America. While there was no specific category for Tuva, several Mongolians and "others" had come to the United States in any given year.

Just in case one of those "others" was from Tuva and had ended up in Los Angeles, I obtained a personalized license plate and mounted it in a do-it-yourself frame with the words "Mongol Motors" and "Kyzyl" flanking "TOUVA" above and below. At the very least, a stamp collector might recognize the spelling and honk if he loved Tuvan postage stamps.

An article I found at the same library at USC claimed that Kyzyl was the USSR's "Atom City"—the center of Soviet atomic weapons development—because Tuva is isolated and surrounded by mountains rich in uranium. Another article, in the *Christian Science Monitor* (September 15, 1966), said:

> According to the official version, Tannu Tuva . . . asked for admission into the Soviet Union. Its "petition was granted," just as four years earlier those of the three Baltic republics had been granted.
>
> In the case of Tannu Tuva the discovery of a large uranium deposit, the first to be found in the Soviet Union on the

threshold of the atomic age, seems to have caused the change of status.

If Kyzyl is the USSR's Los Alamos, I thought, then the KGB will never believe that Richard Feynman wants to visit the place because of how it is spelled!

In the summer of 1978, after competing in the First Annual Southern California Clown Diving Championships in Los Angeles, I flew to Europe for a camping trip in the Balkans. Meanwhile, Richard went to the doctor complaining of abdominal pains. He soon underwent surgery. The doctor removed a fourteen-pound mass of cancer the size of a football that had crushed his kidney and spleen. Richard needed the remainder of the summer to recover.

When I returned from Europe, there was no reply from my fellow teachers at Shkola No. 2 or Shkola No. 1.

In the fall a new school year began, this time without the coaching responsibilities. Another change: along with four math classes, I was permitted to teach one class of world geography. Of course my students eventually learned about a little lost country called Tannu Tuva, but there were more important things to discuss: the horrors of the Khmer Rouge regime in Cambodia were becoming known to the outside world; Iran was in turmoil, with the Shah's regime threatened by the exiled Muslim leader Ayatollah Khomeini; and Pope John Paul I had died after thirty-three days in office and was succeeded by Karol Cardinal Wojtyla of Poland, the first non-Italian pope in four hundred years. In the Middle East, Moammar Kadafi was angry with Anwar Sadat for signing the Camp David Accords with Menachem Begin. (I therefore had to explain why the geography book, written in the 1960s, said that Libya and Egypt were allies against Israel.)

Although there was no ballet to work on in 1978, Richard and I continued drumming together. When we discussed

Tuva, it was usually connected with a letter I had written, perhaps to a college or library in the United States or in England. But one time it was Richard who had something to report: he showed me a little article he had found in the *Los Angeles Times*—one of those fillers that takes up one or two inches—that said a Scythian gold sculpture depicting a hunter, his dog, and a wild boar had been found in the Tuva ASSR.

"I've been meaning to write to Radio Moscow," I said. "They have a program called 'Moscow Mailbag.' I'll ask them about the Scythian gold sculpture—maybe they have a picture of it."

During Christmas vacation I went to Washington, D.C., to visit an old high school friend. While I was there I went to the Library of Congress. The card catalog revealed a gold mine of books on Tuva. Because people off the street are not allowed into the stacks, I presented a dozen slips of paper containing call numbers to a clerk. Half an hour later, only six books were waiting for me—the other six were not to be found. Was someone else onto Tuva?

A senior librarian informed me that it was common for books to be misplaced, and that finding only six out of twelve books was not unusual.

My frustration faded when I looked at the books that *had* been located. Among them were three gems. The first was a pocket-sized Tuvan-Mongolian-Russian phrasebook. The second gem was much larger—a book by Otto Mänchen-Helfen called *Reise ins asiatische Tuwa*. The photographs in this book looked like the scenes in the famous Tuvan postage stamps of the 1930s. Because the book was published in 1931, this was understandable. (In fact, when I looked at my stamps later, I noticed that the picture on the diamond-shaped 3-kopek stamp of 1936 seemed to have been lifted straight out of Mänchen-Helfen's book, only it was reversed.)

When I looked at the first paragraph of *Reise ins asiatische*

The photographs in Otto Mänchen-Helfen's book *Reise ins asiatische Tuwa* (Berlin, 1931) reminded us of Tuva's famous postage stamps from the 1930s. In one case, the connection was more direct than we first thought. (Courtesy Dr. Anna Maenchen)

Tuwa, years of suffering through high school German were
rewarded at last: I was able to follow along enough to get the
point. (The translation here has been provided by my
brother, Alan.)

> An eccentric Englishman of the kind Jules Verne loved as a
> hero traveled the world with the sole purpose of erecting a
> memorial stone at the midpoint of each continent: "I was here
> at the center of the continent on this day"—and the date.
> Africa and North and South America already had their stones
> when he set out to put a monument in the heart of Asia.
> According to his calculations, it lay on the banks of the upper
> Yenisei in the Chinese region of Urianghai. A rich sports-
> man, tough (as many fools are), he braved every hardship and
> reached his goal. I saw the stone in the summer of 1929. It
> stands in Saldam, in Tuva (as the former Urianghai is now
> called), in the herdsmen's republic, which lies between Si-
> beria, the Altai Mountains, and the Gobi: the Asian land least
> accessible to Europeans.[2]

So there *was* someone else onto Tuva—we had a soul mate
from the nineteenth century!

The third gem at the Library of Congress was small and
thin, some sort of guidebook written in Russian. From the
charts and numbers I could tell there was a lot of talk about
increased output of this and that—the usual "progress under
socialism" stuff. There was also a map of Kyzyl, with drawings
of various buildings. I immediately recognized the new government building, the regional Party headquarters, the post
office, and the hotel; there was also a drama theater. A trolley
bus line ran from the airport right into the center of town. I

---

[2]*Reise ins asiatische Tuwa* was so interesting that I persuaded Alan to translate the
whole book. His translation can be obtained through Friends of Tuva (see Appendix
C), or from Ethnographics Press, University of Southern California, Los Angeles,
CA 90089-0032.

made a Xerox copy of the map to show to Richard when I got back to California.

The small book also contained a crude map of the whole country, with little silhouettes of various animals: in the northeast there were foxes and reindeer; in the south, camels; and in the west there were yaks—all within 150 miles of Kyzyl. I thought, Here's this wide variety of animals again. Maybe the Tuva shown on the stamps of 1936 and in Mänchen-Helfen's book can still be found outside of Kyzyl today.

As a visitor to the Library of Congress I was not allowed to borrow the books; I would have to order them later through my local library. With trepidation I relinquished them to be "reshelved," perhaps to be lost forever.

When I got back to California and went through my mail, there was a reply from Radio Moscow: while they had no information on the Scythian gold sculpture found in Tuva, they did say that Tuva would be featured in the weekly series "Round About the Soviet Union" on January 17, only a few weeks away. I thought, How lucky we were to write just when we did—I don't listen to Radio Moscow much; we surely would have missed it!

On January 3, two weeks before the program of interest to us, I tuned in "Round About the Soviet Union" to check which frequency had the best signal. The announcer said, "This week's program features Kamchatka. . . ."

A week later I tuned in again. This time the announcer said, "This week's program is about the Moldavian Soviet Socialist Republic. . . ."

On January 17, after dinner, Richard came over. We drummed awhile. My timer went *ding!*—it was 9 P.M., fifteen minutes before the program. I switched on the shortwave radio and tuned in Radio Moscow. The signal was strong.

As the announcer read a news bulletin, I got out the map of

downtown Kyzyl I had copied at the Library of Congress. On the floor we spread out the present that Alan had given me for Christmas—a large, detailed map of Tuva (Operational Navigation Chart E-7) published by the U.S. Defense Mapping Agency. It showed elevation contours, vegetation patterns, lakes, rivers, dams, and—because the map was made primarily for pilots—deviations of magnetic north from true north, the length and direction of airport runways, and the location and height of radio towers.

It was time for the program to begin, so I switched on my tape recorder. The announcer said, "The topic for this week's program was selected by listener Ralph Leighton of Altadena, California. Today we will go to Tuva, located in the heart of Asia. . . ."

"Fantastic! They made the program just for us!" cried Richard.

Most of the broadcast was information I had already found in the *Great Soviet Encyclopedia* at the San Francisco library— but with the names of some provinces misread, and several directions wrong. But then came a story we had never heard: in the past, shamans made coats and boots out of asbestos (called "mountain wool" in Tuvan, I later found out), which enabled them to dance on hot coals—thus demonstrating their extraordinary powers.

Then came the Party line about how Tuva joined the USSR in 1944, and how everything is hunky-dory under socialism. Finally the narrator said, "Although Tuva was isolated from the outside world in the past, it is now easy to reach. Today, one can fly comfortably from Moscow to Kyzyl by jet."

The announcer mentioned my name again as the music faded out. We were ecstatic.

"Tuva is easy to reach!" said Richard. "They said it themselves!"

We immediately began outlining a letter to Radio Moscow.

I was ready to propose that Altadena and Kyzyl become sister cities, but Richard kept me on the straight by reminding me of our goal: "All we have to do is thank Radio Moscow for the program, remind them of what they said about Tuva being easy to reach, and then ask them to help us get there."

I was so excited that the next day I played the tape for my geography class without stopping to think that any student could have reported to the principal that "Mr. Leighton played Radio Moscow to his class." (It was 1979: the Cold War was still going strong, things Russian were definitely *not* chic, and teachers still had to sign loyalty oaths.) I even played the tape to my math classes. Among my students were two Armenians from Yerevan who knew some Russian. Now that Tuva was "easy to reach," I asked them to translate a letter addressed to "Hotel, Kyzyl, Tuva ASSR," asking for room rates.

A few days later I finished my letter to Radio Moscow. In addition to thanking them for producing the program just for me, I played up the fact that I was a geography teacher, and my students knew all about Tuva now. Then I reminded Radio Moscow that according to their program, Tuva is "easy to reach," and popped the question: "Might it be possible that I could visit Tuva myself?" (We figured the professor of physics could be added later, once the geography teacher got permission to go.)

I knew what we were getting into: Radio Moscow would interview us after our trip to Tuva, editing our answers so that only positive things came out, but I figured it was a price we could afford. Nobody listens to Radio Moscow, I rationalized. Otherwise, the programs about Kamchatka and Moldavia would have begun with a listener's name, as ours did.

While we were waiting for Radio Moscow's reply—a period marked by the radiation leak at Three Mile Island and the election of Margaret Thatcher—Alan gave me a page Xeroxed from the *World Radio and Television Handbook,* the bible of shortwave listening. Listed under 3995 kHz were two stations—Yuzhno-Sakhalinsk (on Sakhalin Island), and Kyzyl. As it was winter the lower frequencies were carrying well in the northern hemisphere, so I set my alarm clock to 3:55 A.M. for a few nights and tuned in 3995 kHz, hoping to catch Radio Tuva's time signal and station ID at 4 A.M.

Most of the time I got one time signal—presumably Yuzhno-Sakhalinsk, since at 5000 miles it was 1200 miles closer to Los Angeles than Kyzyl. (I couldn't be sure, however, since shortwave signals bounce off the ionosphere in strange ways.) But one night I got two signals, one faint and one loud. The fainter one said something like "Rabeet Tivah" before it was drowned out by the louder one.

I played a tape of "Rabeet Tivah" to Mary Zirin, who thought the words might be "Govorit Tuva" ("Tuva speaking"), a plausible way for radio stations to identify themselves in Russian. That prompted me to send a reception report to Kyzyl.

While I was holding my breath for a QSL card from Radio Tuva,[3] three books arrived from the Library of Congress—the gems had not been lost. I immediately copied each book on the best machine I could find, and promptly sent them back to Washington. With the gracious help of Mary Zirin, the Tuvan-Mongolian-Russian phrasebook became a Tuvan-Mongolian-Russian-English phrasebook.

It was a useful little book, with statements such as "I am a teacher," and questions like "Do you have a Russian-Mongolian dictionary?" It was also revealing: "How do you deliver goods to the shepherds?" indicated that shepherds in Tuva were still rather isolated in 1972, when the book was published. There were single words for "spring camp," "summer camp," "fall camp," and "winter camp," allowing us to imag-

---

[3]"QSL" is ham radio lingo for "I acknowledge receipt." A QSL card sent by a radio station acknowledges receipt of a listener's (correct) reception report.

ine that Tuvans were still moving with their animals from one pasture to another according to the season. There was also evidence of modernization: "How do you carry out the breeding of a cow?"—"We have adopted artificial insemination by hand insertion."

As for city life, the question "How many rooms are there in your apartment?" was answered with "I have a comfortable apartment." (Obviously a touchy subject: there must be a housing shortage in Kyzyl.)

In a section entitled "Government Institutions and Social Organizations" came an interesting series of phrases: "Comrades, I declare the meeting to be opened!"—"Chairman of the meeting"—"Agenda for the day"—"To vote"—"To raise one's hand"—"Who is against?"—"Who abstains?"—"It is approved unanimously."

There were single words for "national wrestling" and "freestyle wrestling," for "horse races," and for "a bow-and-arrow horse race." There were no fewer than thirteen words and phrases describing the horses themselves—in terms of appearance, age, function, and behavior. The prime Tuvan delicacy was described as "fat of lamb's tail." There was also the useful phrase, "Is it possible to obtain a collection of works of folklore?"

The little phrasebook had a whole section on greetings, which gave us the idea of writing a letter in Tuvan. When we got to the body of the letter—the "I would like to go to Tuva" part—we began to mix and match: in this case, we used "I would like to meet with Comrade S" and "They want to go to the theater," substituting "Tuva" for "the theater." But it was tricky. We gradually deduced that English is written backwards in relation to Tuvan: word for word, the Tuvan phrases were "I Comrade S-with meet-to-like-would I" and "They theater-to go-to-want they." (Tuvan seemed to have a Department of Redundancy Department for personal pronouns.)

If we needed a particular word that was not in the phrasebook, we used the pocket English-Russian dictionary to get us into Russian, and then a Russian-Tuvan dictionary (borrowed from UCLA) to get us into Tuvan. Then we used a Tuvan-Russian dictionary followed by the Russian-English dictionary to check our choice. We often came out with a different word, necessitating a new choice in Russian and/or Tuvan.

By the time we were finished, we had managed to put together about ten sentences. In addition to saying "I Tuva-to go-to-like-would I," I asked if there were any Tuvan-English or English-Tuvan dictionaries, any schoolbooks in Tuvan, or any recordings of spoken Tuvan.

At last we were ready to send off our masterpiece—but to whom? Richard noticed some small print at the back of the phrasebook: it was written by the Tuvan Scientific Research Institute of Language, Literature, and History (its acronym in Russian was TNIIYaLI), on 4 Kochetova Street, 667000 Kyzyl, Tuva ASSR—a precise address, ZIP code and all!

About a month later a letter from the USSR arrived—not my coveted QSL card from Radio Tuva, but a reply from Radio Moscow. Miss Eugenia Stepanova wrote, "I called up the Intourist travel agency and was told that since they have no offices in Tuva, there are no trips for foreign tourists to that region." Tuva might be easy to reach for a Muscovite, but we Americans were still back on square one. (We should have known better than to believe everything we heard on Radio Moscow!)

I refused to be deterred. "If there's no Intourist office in Tuva," I reasoned, "then why not get them to open one?" I devised a plan:

1. I write a travel article about the fascinating postage-stamp land of Tuva, sounding as if I had already been to the place (I would write it in the form "when one goes here" and "when one goes there"), and submit it to various travel magazines.

2. A travel magazine prints the article, which tells the reader how to arrange travel to Tuva: "Contact the Soviet travel agency Intourist." (An address would be supplied.)
3. We get every friend we can think of from all over the United States to send a letter to Intourist saying they have read about Tuva in the travel magazine and want further information.
4. Responding to this "popular demand," Intourist opens an office in Kyzyl. (Never mind that only two guys actually end up going to Tuva, and the office closes one month later.)

Richard shook his head in dismay, but he couldn't talk me out of this one. I wrote an article called "Journey to the Fifth Corner of the World," and sent it off to half a dozen travel magazines.

The plan never made it past step one.

Still undeterred, I thought: If we can't get Intourist to open an office in Tuva, then where is the nearest place that already has an office? Answer: Abakan, 262 miles to the northwest of Kyzyl, according to the automobile atlas of the USSR I had picked up in Bulgaria during my camping trip in the Balkans. Intourist had rental cars in Abakan. We could drive from there to Shushenskoye, a village—now sacred—where Lenin had been exiled under the Czar; the turnoff is 40 miles along the road to Tuva. We would simply miss the turnoff and drive like hell for 222 more miles. Even if we got stuck behind a truck, we could easily reach Kyzyl by nightfall—especially in summer, when the sun sets around 10 P.M. From Kyzyl we would telephone Abakan and say we had gotten lost.

Richard was completely opposed to that plan, because it was deceptive. Acting under false pretenses was one of the biggest sins in his book.

In the summer of 1979 Jimmy Carter and Leonid Brezhnev signed the SALT II Treaty. Meanwhile I wrote more letters in Tuvan, this time to *Bashky* (teacher), at *Shkola* (there seemed to be no Tuvan word for "school"), in remote towns with

Tuvan names where (according to a map of Soviet nationalities I had found at UCLA) the majority of Tuvans live.

I also continued my research in libraries around Southern California. I found an article in the *Times* of London (November 23, 1970) written by a fellow named Owen Lattimore, who had gone to Tuva on his way to Mongolia. He was apparently the first Westerner to visit Tuva since Otto Mänchen-Helfen, more than forty years before. Lattimore's article concluded with this paragraph:

> And lastly, the Tuvinians[4] themselves. They are the most captivating of the minority people that I have yet encountered in the Soviet Union. Mostly of middle height, they commonly have oval faces, a rather finely marked nose with delicate nostrils, often slightly tilted eyes. They are elegant, gay, assured. They love good food and drink, and wide-ranging conversation with a light touch; but their academic style, in the fields with which I am acquainted, is precise and rigorous. I lost my heart to Tuva and its people.

Naturally, I tracked down Lattimore's address in England and asked how he had been able to get into Tuva. He replied in a handwritten letter that he had gone as a guest of the Siberian Center of the Soviet Academy of Sciences, and that his trip had been arranged in Novosibirsk. It wasn't until several years afterward that I realized the answer to my naive inquiry had come from "God" himself—the dean of Central Asian studies.[5]

Soon after that I began receiving a publication called the *Central Asian Newsletter* from England. Apparently, during

---

[4]Lattimore used an anglicized Russian word for "Tuvans."

[5]Owen Lattimore (1900–1989) was an American author and scholar who had the singular distinction of being in good standing with the Soviets, the Mongols, and the Chinese—both in Beijing and in Taipei—but emotional debate over his political views raged on even after his death. (See the June 9, July 11, and July 25, 1989, editions of the *New York Times.*) He had been living in England since 1963.

the course of my inquiries to colleges and universities, someone had put me on their mailing list as a specialist. My enthusiasm was further boosted by a letter from Dr. Thomas E.
Ewing of the University of Leeds, which began, "It is a pleasure to welcome you to Tuvan studies—your appearance
alone must double the population of the field."

In the fall of 1979 another school year began. Again, serious world events were discussed in my geography class: Vietnam invaded Cambodia and chased the murderous dictator
Pol Pot into exile; President Park Chung Hee of South Korea
was assassinated; and in November, Iranian militants seized
the U.S. embassy in Tehran and captured more than fifty
hostages.

Then, over Christmas vacation, the Red Army invaded
Afghanistan. The eminent Soviet physicist Andrei Sakharov,
who had formed a committee in Moscow to monitor the
USSR's compliance with the Helsinki Accords on Human
Rights, publicly condemned the invasion. Leonid Brezhnev
deported him to Gorky, a city closed to foreigners. Sakharov,
in a letter smuggled out to the West, called on the nations of
the world to boycott the Olympic Games, which were going
to be held in Moscow that summer. President Carter, who
had made human rights the centerpiece of his foreign policy,
announced that the United States would honor the boycott.

As 1980 began, Richard and I realized that we hadn't made
any progress toward our goal. With U.S.-Soviet relations
deteriorating by the day, we figured our chances of reaching
Kyzyl had slipped from slim to none.

Nevertheless, I continued looking for books about Tuva in
various local libraries. In one of them I found a photograph
taken in Kyzyl that made my heart throb: a tall obelisk with a
globe underneath, sitting on a base inscribed with the words
TSENTR AZII, AZIANYNG TÖVÜ, and THE CENTRE
OF ASIA—obviously inspired by our soul mate, that eccentric English traveler described in Mänchen-Helfen's book. I

showed the photograph to Richard. The monument to the "Centre of Asia" became our Holy Grail.

At another library I also struck it rich: there was a new book out, called the *Tuvan Manual*, by John R. Krueger, a professor at Indiana University. The book was packed with information—over seventy-five pages on Tuvan geography, history, economics, and culture—as well as a detailed description of the Tuvan language.

In a section called "Folk Art" we encountered these intriguing words:

A characteristic and specific feature of Tuvan music is the so-called two-voiced solo or "throat" singing commonly found among native Tuvans and hardly observed anywhere else. The singer sings in two voices. With his lower voice he sings the melody and accompanies it at the same time with a surprisingly pure and tender sound similar to that of the flute.

The only kind of throat singing I was familiar with was the bizarre imitation of animal sounds practiced by Inuit women of northern Quebec, which I had heard a few years before on Radio Canada. But a solo singer producing two notes *at the same time* sounded not just bizarre; it sounded impossible! This we had to see—and hear—for ourselves.

Another intriguing statement in the *Tuvan Manual* had to do with pronunciation: "Although adopting the term 'glottalized vowels' in this book, one remains uncertain as to exactly what the articulatory and phonetic nature of these sounds is." In other words, Tuvan was such an obscure language that the author hadn't heard it spoken.

Professor Krueger's book contained several examples of written Tuvan, a Tuvan-English glossary, and a sixteen-page bibliography, including a listing of Columbia University holdings of books written in the Tuvan language. The *Tuvan Manual* became our bible.

At the end of January, I found a strange letter in my mailbox: it was addressed to "RALPH LEISHTOH, 248 N. PAGE DR., ALTADENA, CALIFORNIA USA 91001."[6] I looked at the postmark: it was in Russian script; it looked like K, 61, 3, 61, upside-down U. But I knew what it was: K-Y-Z-Y-L. A letter from Kyzyl!

I didn't open it. I would wait until Richard was home.

That night I went over to the Feynmans', letter in hand. Richard was surprised and excited. We opened it together.

It was dated 7.1.1980, which we deduced to mean January 7, since July 1 hadn't come around yet. It was from the TNIIYaLI, the Tuvan Scientific Research Institute of Language, Literature, and History, which had written the Tuvan-Mongolian-Russian phrasebook.

All I could make out was my name, which was in the first sentence. So Richard and I went over to my place and looked at the Tuvan-Mongolian-Russian phrasebook. The first word of the letter, "Ekii," was the third phrase in the book: it meant "Hello." So the first sentence was "Hello, Ralph Leighton!" But then the phrasebook was of no use: the phrases were arranged according to subject, not in alphabetical order.

"We can't expect everything to be written just like it is in the phrasebook, anyway," said Richard. "This letter is written in *real* Tuvan—not fake Tuvan, like ours was."

Richard got out our Xeroxed copy of the Tuvan-Russian dictionary, and I got out my pocket Russian-English dictionary, as well as the *Tuvan Manual.* Word by word, we deciphered the second sentence: "New Year with!" So the second sentence was equivalent to "Happy New Year!"

The third sentence came out "Me Daryma Ondar called, forty-five snowy I."

---

[6]My name is LEIGHTON and my address was 2484 N. Page Dr., etc. I no longer live there. The address for those wishing to correspond is: Box 70021, Pasadena, California 91117 USA. (See Appendix C.)

We couldn't make head nor tail of "forty-five snowy I."

"Imagine you were a Navajo living on a reservation in New Mexico," said Richard, beginning to laugh. "And one day, out of the blue, you get this letter written in broken Navajo from a guy in Russia using a Navajo-Spanish-English phrase-book that he got translated into Russian by a friend of his. So you write back to him in *real* Navajo . . ."

"No wonder it's hard to read real Tuvan," I said.

Then Richard suddenly said, "Hey! I've got it: the guy is forty-five years old."

It made perfect sense. It was something like saying, "I have survived forty-five winters"—an apt phrase for Tuva, which lies between Siberia and Mongolia.

We checked the dictionaries again. There was a second definition for "snowy" that came out *letnii* in Russian—"summer" in English!

"Winters, summers, what does it matter?" said Richard. "It still could mean he has lived forty-five years."

Then I looked carefully through the phrasebook again. At the bottom of page 32 was the question "How old are you?" And at the top of page 33 was the answer: "*dörten besh kharlyg men*"—"forty-five snowy I."

Mysterious Melodies

WE struggled happily for a week to translate the rest of Ondar Daryma's letter, word by word. It came out like this: **3**

Your written-having letter-your reading acquainted I. [I found out about your letter and read it.] Tuva-in written-having-your gladness full-am-I. [I'm glad you wrote in Tuvan.] Our Tuvan language Turk language-to related-is. [Tuvan is related to Turkish.] You-to letter reached? [Did this letter reach you?—A rather odd question, we thought, since there was only one possible answer.] Whom-from letter taking-are-you? [Whom are you corresponding with?] Our institute-from letter took-you? [Are you corresponding with someone at our institute?]

Daryma's letter continued:

Kyzyl town-in book stores are. Russian-Tuvan and Tuvan-Russian dictionaries book are. Tuva's center

Kyzyl town. Asia's center spot our nice, clean town-our-in. Stay-to days-for its environs-from people break not. [The best sense we could make out of that was: When people stay in Kyzyl's environs for several days, they can't tear themselves away.] Us-by Tuvan-English dictionary book not. Record-in written song, tune is. What interested-in are you? Us-to letter-from write-you.

The last paragraph read:

I this institute-in Tuva folk mouth literary collect writing am I. [That sentence rang a bell—the phrase, "Is it possible to obtain a collection of works of folklore?" The collector himself was writing to us!] Fifteen years working still-am I. Following letter writing your waiting am I. Great-abundant be-to-you-with wish-I. Big-with full-am-I. [That phrase was under the section entitled "gratitude": it meant "I am full of big thanks."]

We were so excited at deciphering Ondar's letter that we didn't notice for several weeks his omission of how one might visit Tuva.

As I began to collect phrases to include in our reply, Richard thumbed through the *Tuvan Manual.* Suddenly he said, "Hey, Ralph, look at this: there's a book in the Columbia University library called *Tyva Tooldar,* edited by O. K. Daryma and K. X. Orgu."

I looked at Ondar's letter: his full name was Ondar Kish-Chalaevich Daryma.

Tyva Tooldar (Tuvan Tales), the last book in the bibliography, was described as "another folklore volume." But its author, O. K. Daryma, was to us not just another folklorist.

A few weeks later our reply was ready. I introduced Richard to Ondar; we mentioned the Tuvan-Mongolian-Russian phrasebook as the source of our Tuvan, and said we were interested in geography and folk cultures, citing the stamps of

1936 that showed yurts, cattle, reindeer, camels, yaks, wrestling, horse racing, and archery. We asked, "Tuva-in these
things still today are?"

Then we mentioned the mysterious "throat" singing by its
proper Tuvan name, *höömei*, and asked whether there were
any recordings of it. Ondar's letter had said, "Record-in written song, tune is," so we thought we might get a positive
response on this one.

Richard wrote his own addition to our letter, saying that he
saw Daryma's book listed at the Columbia University library
in New York. Under his name he drew a motif that he had
seen in a book about Tuva.

We sent the letter off in mid-February, hoping that we
would get a reply more quickly than before: the answer to our
first letter had taken nearly a year!

"I wonder what the delay was," I said. "It took only three
weeks for Ondar's letter to reach us; could it have taken nine
months for our letter to reach him?"

"Maybe it took Ondar nine months to figure out what we
were trying to say," said Richard.

I smiled. Then I thought of something. "Hey, I know: it's
the FBI. Here's this envelope addressed to Kyzyl, the USSR's
'Atom City,' so the FBI opens it. The letter inside is written in
the Russian alphabet, but it's not Russian—it must be some
kind of code. It takes the FBI nine months to figure out that
the letter is written in fractured Tuvan."[1]

---

[1]Why not the KGB? That would be more likely if a Russian wrote letters in Navajo
and sent them to Los Alamos—in which case it might take the KGB nine months to
figure out that those letters were not written in code either. Furthermore, I recently
requested my FBI file under the Freedom of Information Act. I was denied access to
fifteen pages of my sixteen-page file (everything was crossed out with a felt pen except
for my Altadena address) because the material was "specifically authorized under
criteria established by an Executive order to be kept secret in the interest of national
defense or foreign policy. . . ."—in my opinion, bureaucratese for, "The government
opened your mail, but doesn't want to admit it." (Of course my file now will grow to
seventeen pages . . .)

As spring gave way to the summer of 1980, the U.S. boy-cott of the Moscow Olympic Games rudely reminded us that our dream of reaching Tuva was not going to be realized any time soon.

In the fall I began a new teaching assignment at a different school in Pasadena. (No geography class this time.) Drum-ming sessions punctuated by Richard's storytelling continued to provide pleasure every week. All was quiet on the Tuvan front.

In November 1980 Ronald Reagan was elected president. His campaign was full of tough talk, much of it against the Soviet Union. Around Thanksgiving I suddenly got the idea that our chances of getting to Tuva weren't necessarily related *directly* to how well the United States and the USSR were getting along; our chances could just as well be related *in-versely:* if relations between the United States and the USSR are so bad, why not offer to help improve them—by going to Tuva, of course!

I wrote a letter to Radio Moscow, TASS (the Soviet news agency), and Intourist describing what an irresistible place Tuva was, and proposed that I write an article about it for the *National Geographic* or *Geo*. Richard would accompany me as the photographer, of course.

Intourist responded promptly: "Thank you for a pleasant and very interesting letter. We regret to inform you that the subject area is beyond Intourist travel routes; therefore we cannot arrange such a visit." Radio Moscow answered later, and referred me to Intourist. TASS never did reply.

As 1980 drew to a close, John Lennon was killed in New York. Fifty-two U.S. hostages were still in Iran, more than one year after they had been seized. Soviet troops marked their first anniversary in Afghanistan. Despite the gloomy state of affairs in the world, Richard and I continued our efforts to maintain contact with Tuva. We sent Ondar a picture book of California and wished him a Happy New Year.

January of 1981 brought Ronald Reagan into office, but it didn't bring a letter from Kyzyl into my mailbox as it had the year before. With our minds on Ondar Daryma, Richard and I remembered his book, *Tyva Tooldar*. A day or two later the Caltech library sent off a loan request to Columbia University for a certain book in Tuvan.

A few weeks later, *Tyva Tooldar* arrived. We immediately Xeroxed it, and looked for a suitable story to translate. There were eighteen to choose from; we began with the shortest story—one page—called "Tarbagan bile Koshkar" ("The Marmot and the Ram"). We couldn't even begin to make out the first sentence. After the first paragraph there appeared to be some sort of dialogue between the two animals about "existence" and "taking things" from the forest. We gave up.

The next shortest story—one and a half pages—was called "Kuskun bile Ügü" ("The Raven and the Eagle Owl"). That jarred my memory; I had seen a Siberian eagle owl at the Los Angeles Zoo.

The story began with the words "Shyian am," which came out "Thus now."

"That doesn't make any sense," I said.

Richard looked at the beginning of the other Tuvan stories. Half of them began with the words "Shyian am" or "Shyian." He said, "Perhaps it's a typical Tuvan way of beginning a story. Suppose we were to look up 'once upon a time,' word by word—it would come out as 'one time,' 'on,' 'one,' and 'an indefinite duration in which things happen.' 'Thus now' makes just as much sense."

We went on to the next sentence. It came out "Early previous very freeze long ago things this way."

The story of the raven and the eagle owl availed itself

more willingly to decipherment (at least so we thought); it took only twenty hours or so, spread over several weeks. It seems a raven and an eagle owl met up one day in the forest and got into an argument over who knew more "languages." The eagle owl claimed nine, and proceeded to imitate the cries of a young child and a fox. The raven claimed seventy-one languages, imitating everything from chickens and vultures to cattle, horses, and gophers. (Tuvan gophers make sounds?)

At any rate, the two birds called each other all sorts of nasty names until they wouldn't have anything more to do with each other. And that is why the raven is seen only in the daytime, and the eagle owl only at night.

Our success at deciphering this Tuvan tale inspired us to write another letter to Ondar Daryma. With words adapted from the phrasebook and from his previous letter, we asked whether he could read "The Raven and the Eagle Owl" into a tape recorder so we could hear what Tuvan sounded like. (We could even make a contribution to the field by sending the recording to Professor Krueger, author of the *Tuvan Manual*, who apparently had never heard the language.)

We also became a bit bolder in stating our desire to visit Kyzyl: we wrote a phrase that came out as, "Asia's center point days-for its environs-in stay-to like-would-we. You-to great satisfaction-with meet we!"

We sent the letter off in March.

A few days later, Richard called me up. "Hey, man," he said, "what latitude and longitude is Tuva?"

"Around 52° North and about 95° East. Why?"

"I'm going to a costume party. This year the requirements are that the costumes be traditional, and from an area between latitudes 40° North and 10° South, and between longitudes 30° and 150° East. I wanted to go as a Tuvan lama."

I quickly got out my atlas. "Too bad they didn't give you

ten more degrees of latitude," I said. "There's a tiny bit of Tuva that's below 50° North."

"Yeah. I guess the best I can do is Tibet."

"That wouldn't be so bad; Tuvan lamas probably looked a lot like Tibetan lamas anyway."

Gweneth was an accomplished seamstress—she made elaborate costumes for Carl and Michelle each Halloween—so she set about looking through *National Geographic* magazines for an article on Tibet. Right away she found an article on Ladakh, a remote Himalayan region steeped in Lamaist traditions. Ladakhi costumes are quite distinctive, with pointed ear flaps sticking out prominently on each side of the hat. Ladakh it would be.

Richard went to the local army surplus store and bought a small circular bearing. He slipped the bearing around a wooden sofa leg that he had bought at a hardware store, jammed a tin can around the bearing, and attached a small chain to the can. At the end of the chain he hung a weight (a miniature Coca-Cola can taken from a key ring), and voilà—a lama's prayer wheel. (The weight on the chain made it possible for the lama to turn his prayer wheel—actually a cylinder—by wobbling his wrist.) One revolution of the prayer wheel equaled one utterance of the prayer inside—a highly efficient way of fulfilling one's spiritual duties while herding yaks.

Richard wanted his prayer wheel to look authentic. "Where can I find some Tibetan writing?" he asked.

"I have a copy of *China Pictorial* in Tibetan," I said. (I had bought it in Chinatown along with editions in English, Chinese, Mongolian, and Uighur.) Pressed for time, Richard copied out the antithesis of a prayer in Tibetan that probably said something like, "May the guiding light of Chairman Mao shine brightly for eternity!"

The costumes were a great success. Richard reported that

Richard dressed up as a Ladakhi lama, complete with prayer wheel. (Courtesy Friends of Tuva.)

when he and Gweneth arrived at the party, a woman gasped, "Ladakh! You're from Ladakh! How on earth did you ever get those costumes out?"[2]

Around the same time I, too, broadened my horizons a bit. Some Japanese friends took me to see *Dersu Uzala*, a joint Soviet-Japanese production directed by Akira Kurosawa. This film marked a distinct change from Kurosawa's previous work: for one thing, it was in color. For another, the story didn't take place in Japan, but in eastern Siberia. Finally, it didn't star Toshiro Mifune; instead, it employed Soviet actors. *Dersu Uzala* had won the Academy Award for best foreign film of 1975.

The film is about a surveying party mapping the Russo-Chinese border at the turn of the twentieth century. Some burly, boisterous young Russian soldiers encounter Dersu, a diminutive hunter, who scolds them for their profligate ways. In a harrowing scene, Dersu saves the life of the team's leader when a fierce windstorm kicks up overnight on a frozen lake.

With my one-track mind, I imagined that Dersu was a Tuvan, even though the movie said he was from the "Goldi" tribe.[3]

Shortly after that grand cinematic experience, Mary Zirin sent me the name of a book she had seen in a brochure from Cambridge University Press: *Nomads of South Siberia*. She knew the book was about Tuva from its Russian title: *Istoricheskaya etnografiya tuvintsev (Historical Ethnography of the Tuvans)*, by Sevyan Vainshtein. We immediately sent away for it.

[2]Pasadena artist Sylvia Posner painted Richard's official Caltech portrait from a photograph of him in that costume. A black-and-white picture of Posner's painting appears at the end of this book.
[3]While furtively searching through the stacks of the earthquake-damaged San Francisco Public Library for the book that had captivated Richard (*Road to Oblivion* by Vladimir Zenzinov—see Footnote 1 on p. 20), I encountered in the same section ("Siberia—description and travel") *Dersu the Trapper* by Vladimir K. Arsenev (New York, 1941), the book upon which Kurosawa's film is based.

The front cover displayed a photo of a young man dressed in robes, standing next to a small, spotted horse. On the back cover was a photo of the author standing with three Tuvans outside a yurt. One of the Tuvans wore a feathered headdress and a long, leather cape with dozens of cords hanging from it. In one hand he (or perhaps she—the face was only dimly visible through a curtain of shorter cords) held a large twelve-sided drum with painted spots on its skin; the other hand held a drum beater. Although the caption made no mention of it, we knew what it was: a shaman—a real Tuvan shaman. The photograph was dated 1959.

The book had an extensive introduction by British anthropologist Dr. Caroline Humphrey. It began:

> There are few, if any, detailed first-hand accounts of Inner Asian pastoralism readily available to Western readers. . . . Vainshtein's book is therefore unique in this field. . . .
>
> Tuva presents, in fact, a paradigm of Central and North Asian pastoral economies. The great remoteness of Tuva—it is a group of high valleys at the headwaters of the Yenisei, cut off on all sides by mountains from the surrounding territories of Siberia and North-west Mongolia—has kept its peoples obscured from outside scrutiny until very recently. But a series of field studies by Soviet ethnographers working to some extent independently of one another has made it clear that in Tuva the three most important traditional economic systems of Inner Asia meet together.
>
> The relatively small area of the upper Yenisei basin is highly differentiated ecologically and supports (a) a reindeer-herding and hunting economy in the mountainous forest zones, (b) a small-scale cattle- and horse-herding and hunting economy in the high forest and meadow zone, and (c) a fully fledged complex steppe pastoralism with five or more different kinds of herd in the dry upland steppes of the south and east. What is significant about this is that each of these types is

found among sections of other Inner Asian societies with var-
ied and different linguistic, cultural, and political features.

Vainshtein's book was a detailed description of postage-
stamp Tuva—the Tuva Mänchen-Helfen had visited. It relied
on the census of 1931, carried out by the Tuvan People's
Republic on its tenth anniversary of independence. The census included dozens of categories such as number of households, size of each household, type of shelters each household
had, whether the shelters were permanent or movable, and so
on. Also recorded were economic activities such as herding,
hunting, farming, smithery, jewelry making, and the carving
of stone and wood.[4]

According to Dr. Humphrey, the census of 1931 made
Tuva the only part of Asia with such detailed data about
pre-Soviet life. So Tuva's independence was beneficial not
only to stamp collectors (not to mention the Tuvans themselves), but to anthropologists as well.

There seemed to be another reason that Vainshtein's book
concentrated on Tuva in the 1930s: in 1944 Tuva became
part of the "fraternal" Union of Soviet Socialist Republics,

[4]The census of 1931 reported that 82.2 percent of Tuvans were nomads with set
migratory routes. The number of shifts per year was recorded (four was most common), as well as the distance covered in each shift (the reindeer herders went the
farthest—about 20 miles, on average—while other Tuvans generally moved less than
10 miles from camp to camp). Livestock—including sheep, goats, cattle (with a separate category for steer), horses, camels, yaks, and reindeer (classified by age)—was
counted, available fodder was measured, as was how much arable land each household had at its disposal. It was noted whether a particular household took on extra
cattle for milking or had them milked by others. Under hunting, the census counted
how many households were engaged in that activity, what equipment they had (such
as rifles), and which animals were taken: squirrels accounted for more than 90 percent of the catch, with the rest made up of hares, roe deer, foxes, wolves, musk deer,
and finally sable, the most valuable fur. In addition to hunting, there were separate
categories for fishing and for gathering (plant roots were the favorite); fishing and
digging implements were tallied.

The back jacket of Sevyan Vainshtein's book *Nomads of South Siberia* (Cambridge, 1980) showed that in 1959, at least one shaman still existed in Tuva. (Courtesy Sevyan Vainshtein.)

and therefore—by definition—no longer had a traditional way of life. "Soviet Tuva is a republic of large-scale collectivized agricultural enterprises and modern industry," wrote Vainshtein on the last page of his book. "A socialist economy and culture is fast being developed."

How sad, we thought. But maybe there was hope: could the shaman on the back of Vainshtein's book still be alive?

The final paragraph of Vainshtein's book was ominous:

> In conclusion, I must emphasise that the experience of developing socialism in Tuva, as in the other republics of the USSR—the experience of an extremely successful transition from nomadic to settled forms of economic life—has a general historical significance. It is particularly important for those peoples who, even now, retain a nomadic economy and live in socio-economic conditions similar in many ways to those of pre-revolutionary Tuva.

Those words seemed to be saying that societies anywhere in the world—in Asia, Africa, and Latin America—didn't have to go through a capitalist phase in order to become "socialist" on the Soviet model. But since the last page of Vainshtein's book was the only one with such rhetoric, perhaps that final paragraph was the price of getting published in the USSR.

After reading *Nomads of South Siberia* Richard and I discussed our next move: a letter to Sevyan Vainshtein. Because we were so desperate after more than three years of trying to get to Tuva, I figured this letter should be from Richard only, on a Caltech letterhead. Otherwise, Vainshtein might take it as just another fan letter. To doubly ensure that Vainshtein would take the letter seriously, I suggested that Richard also send regards to some Russian scientists he knew—so they could tell Vainshtein who he was.

We each wrote out what we thought should be in the letter, and then combined, sorted, and edited. The letter read:

Dear Dr. Vainshtein,

Recently I read *Nomads of South Siberia,* the English translation of your book *Istoricheskaya etnografiya tuvintsev.* You have
described very clearly, and in great detail, scenes that I first
saw as a child on Tuvinian postage stamps of the 1930s.

My interest in Tuva was revived a few years ago when a
geography teacher friend and I were discussing remote areas
of the world—and what place fits this description better, we
thought, than the geographical center of Asia! When we
found out that within 150 km of Kyzyl there are mountains
and taiga forests with reindeer, steppes with horses, cattle,
and yaks, and a semi-desert with camels, and all of these areas
populated by Turkic-speaking, shaman/Buddhist, "throat"-
singing, friendly people, we decided, "This place we must
visit!" And we've been trying to do so ever since.

We didn't have the courage to tell Vainshtein that the real
reason we wanted to go to Tuva was the spelling of its capital:
K-Y-Z-Y-L—he'd know we were nuts for sure! The letter continued:

As we expected, Tuva is very difficult to reach, especially
for someone from the USA. Intourist and Radio Moscow
have been kind, but have been of no help. It seems that there
is no one in Moscow who can understand why we would want
to visit Tuva.

After obtaining a copy of the *Tuvinsko-Mongolsko-Ruskii
Razgovornik,* we wrote a letter in Tuvinian to the TNIIYaLI in
Kyzyl, and received a very friendly reply (also in Tuvinian)
from Mr. Ondar Daryma (*Tyva Tooldar,* 1968); we answered
him, but have heard nothing from him since.

We realize that only very rarely do people from the West
obtain permission to visit Tuva. Since you have been there
many times, and know what an interesting place it is, we think
you can understand why *we* would like to visit Tuva.

Do you know of a way that we could arrange a trip to the

Tuvinskaya ASSR? Any suggestions you might have will be greatly appreciated.

Please give my regards to Professor V. B. Braginsky of Moscow University and Professor V. L. Ginzburg at Lebedev University.

Thank you again for a most informative book about this most interesting area of the world.

Sincerely,
Richard Feynman

After we sent off the letter, I had second thoughts about mentioning Braginsky and Ginzburg: they might try to do Richard a "favor" by arranging some lectures in Moscow in exchange for a trip to Tuva (exactly the way that Richard did *not* want to reach our goal), thus putting him in the awkward position of having to refuse something that had taken a lot of effort to set up. Luckily, no such thing happened.

In May the annual Caltech physics picnic was held in the mountains north of Pasadena. Since my father was on the faculty, I had gone nearly every year until I went off to college at UCLA. Now that I had graduated and was teaching in Pasadena, I decided to go and reacquaint myself with old friends. One was Tina Cowan, the daughter of a physics professor, whom I had coached in swimming along with her brother Glen.

It turned out that Glen, now a graduate student in physics at Berkeley, had studied Russian for several years at UCLA. He had even gone to Leningrad to study Russian for six weeks. Perfect, I thought. Glen could check out the big research library at Berkeley. What's more, he could actually understand the many Russian books they are sure to have about Tuva.

When Glen came back to Pasadena for a short visit in June, I went to see him. It didn't take any arm-twisting at all—he took to Tuva like an electron to a proton. He would be spending the summer in the Bay Area working on a physics project at Berkeley and Stanford (another good library!).

In July of 1981 President Reagan chose Sandra Day O'-Connor to become a member of the Supreme Court, and Prince Charles chose Lady Diana Spencer to become a member of the Royal Court.

Then in early August the nation's air traffic controllers, citing impossible working conditions, went on strike—severely disrupting flights all across the country. I had already bought a ticket to Seattle, so I gritted my teeth, blew on my sweaty palms, and had a smooth flight.

While in Seattle visiting my mother, I found an interesting book at the University of Washington library about some rune-like inscriptions found in the valleys of the Orkhon (in Mongolia) and the Yenisei—in Tuva. The "Orkhon-Yenisei inscriptions," written in ancient Turkic, looked remarkably similar to the runes common in Scandinavia, which appeared several centuries later.

Also in the UW library was a book on Tuvan art by Sevyan Vainshtein. The cover featured a beautiful stone carving of a camel. Inside there were several examples of historical art, including a large bronze plaque from Scythian times (eighth century B.C.) of a coiled panther. The last twenty pages of the book showed more stone carvings—yaks, foxes, horses, goats, rams, reindeer, and so on—which seemed to be the principal form of Tuvan artistic expression in the twentieth century.

There was also a book on Tuvan holidays. Some of the celebrations were tied to the lunar calendar observed in China and Mongolia: in Tuva, Lunar New Year was called *Shagaa*; the biggest summer festival was called *Naadym*. Tuvan Independence Day was also in the summer—August 14, 1921. I had just enough time to make a flier commemorating the sixtieth anniversary of Tuvan independence, complete with Tuvan motifs in each corner, framed by a string of Orkhon-Yenisei inscriptions. The text said, "Celebrate the occasion by dusting off that old atlas or stamp collection and saying, 'Tuva is nothing to be sneezed at!' Find out what happened to Tannu Tuva by joining the Friends of Tuva. Send no money, just greetings!"[5]

The anniversary of Tuvan independence also inspired me to write a letter to the State Department. In view of our government's refusal to recognize the Soviet annexation of Latvia, Lithuania, and Estonia, I pointed out that there was a fourth country, also independent between the two world wars, that was annexed in a similar fashion: the Tuvan People's Republic. I asked, "Does the United States recognize the Soviet Union's annexation of Tuva as legitimate and legal?"

I did not receive a reply. Obviously there was not a big enough Tuvan lobby in the United States to force an answer.

I began looking more closely at maps and globes in stores. A piggy-bank globe at K-Mart showed Tannu Tuva as an independent country; a world-map shower curtain in a designer bath boutique had the territory as part of Mongolia, itself portrayed as a province of China. The source of these deviant maps turned out to be Taiwan.

The first page in *Republic of China: A Reference Book* (printed in Taipei) said it officially:

> China is located in continental Asia and nearby islands. . . . Its easternmost boundary is at Longitude 135° 4' E, at the junction of the Amur and Ussuri Rivers; the westernmost boundary, Longitude 71° E on the Pamir Plateau. The southernmost point of China is Latitude 4° N in Nansha Chuntao (the South Sand Islands); and the northernmost point at Latitude 53° 57' N in the Sayan Ridge in northern Tannu Tuva.

That prompted me to write to the government on Taiwan and ask for the name of Tuva's representative, since all the

---

[5]I didn't realize it at the time, but with that flier I inadvertently founded an organization which may yet engage in some serious business. You are invited to join the Friends of Tuva today—see Appendix C.

provinces of old China, including Mongolia, were still represented in Taipei. I resisted asking for a visa to visit Tuva.

(Several months later I received a booklet from the Taiwan
government. I showed it to a Chinese friend, who found
Tuva—called "Tang-nu U-liang-hai"—on the last page, listed
as a "banner" under a Mongolian "flag." I never did find out
the name of Tuva's representative in Taipei, who had probably long since died, anyway.)

While I was still in Seattle, Glen sent a letter reporting on
his Tuva research at Berkeley and Stanford. He listed the
books he had found, and summarized their contents. He
wrote, "As it turns out, you can hardly open a book on Tuva
without finding plenty of mention of this S. I. Vainshtein.
He's apparently quite an authority on Tuvinian ethnographic
studies."

Glen also reported finding *Uchenye Zapiski,* a monograph
series published by Ondar Daryma's institute in Kyzyl, which
contained "an excellent collection of articles on Tuvinian life,
language, music, ethnography, local economy, and, of course,
the latest exciting news on how thrilled to death they are to
have voluntarily entered the Soviet Union."

Then he wrote,

The only non-Russian piece of information on Tuva is a
novel, translated into English, called *A Shepherd's Tale* (Russian—*Slovo Arata*), by Salchak Toka. This is the first third of
an autobiographical trilogy by Tuva's most famous writer, and
is probably his most famous work. From a literary standpoint,
it's horrible. Its perfectly strict adherence to the accepted
propaganda line makes it so predictable it's ridiculous. It cov-
ers his life in the Kaa-Khem region of Tuva from his birth in
1901 through the civil war. (Apparently there were a number
of battles and quite a bit of partisan activity in the area.) It
goes from his life in a decrepit birch-bark "choom" (sort of

like a teepee), oppressed by the rich rulers at every turn, to his first meeting with Russian peasants, whom he finds to be marvelously friendly, talented, and technically advanced people. Passing through a number of adventures it finally winds up with him joining a Red partisan unit in a crucial battle against the Whites. After the battle, the commander lines up his comrades in arms. "He rode to the middle of the ranks and raised his arm: 'Comrades, you have carried the task out magnificently. Allow me to express the appreciation of the Siberian Revolutionary Military Council!'—'We serve Soviet power!' the partisans replied in a chorus."

So ends book one. Actually, it was fun reading, and contained a lot of interesting information on Tuvinian life and history. (The history, however, has to be taken with a certain grain of salt.) I'm looking for books two and three, with no luck so far. There has been a tremendous amount written about *A Shepherd's Tale* (criticism, etc.), and it's been translated into some 21 languages of the peoples of the USSR. I definitely recommend you read it if you haven't already.

Sometime later I realized I had seen that name Toka before. It was in the first chapter of Mänchen-Helfen's book *Reise ins asiatische Tuwa.* The paragraphs about Toka and his fellow students turned out to be quite illuminating:

The Kommunisticheskii Universitet Trudyashchikhsya Vostoka imeni Stalina (the Joseph Stalin Communist University of the Toilers of the East—abbreviated KUTV because one runs out of breath when one has to pronounce this monster of a title a few times) fitted out an expedition in 1929 to investigate the economic conditions and potential of Tuva. The university, on Moscow's Strastnaya Square, is a strange institution. Behind the great red monastery, after which the square is named, stands an inconspicuous two-storey building where human bombs are manufactured. Hundreds of young Orientals—Yakuts, Mongols, Tuvans, Uzbeks, Koreans, Afghans, and Persians—are trained there for three years to ex-

plode the old ways in their homelands. In three years shaman-
ists are turned into atheists, worshippers of Buddha into worshippers of tractors. Equipped with soap, toothbrushes, and
meager Russian, these fine fellows—crammed with catch-
words and slogans and fanaticized, as missionaries surely must
be if they are to accomplish anything—have the mission of
pushing their countrymen straight into the twenty-first century.

In a single month (of which something yet will be told), the
five students with whom I went to Tuva—Sedip-ool, Toka,
Tapit, Chinchig-ool, and the small, clever Kamova[6]
—expelled two-thirds of the Tuvan People's Revolutionary
Party membership and raced madly across the steppes, con-
fiscating all livestock over twenty head from the nomad families in order to set up government herds of camels, sheep,
goats, and cattle—an original way indeed of socializing of the
means of milk production!

On the way back to Pasadena from Seattle, I stopped off in
Berkeley to visit Glen. We decided to go over to the Soviet
consulate in San Francisco and see what the staff there had to
say about going to Tuva.

We found the plain, brick building—with a dozen anten-
nas of every description on the roof—in a fashionable neighborhood near the U.S. Army Presidio, about a mile from the
Golden Gate Bridge. We pressed the button on the gate, and
a buzzer sounded to unlock it. After a few minutes of waiting
in the lobby, browsing through travel brochures on Armenia,
Georgia, and Azerbaijan, we were met by an officer from the
consulate—a pleasant man in his fifties.

We stated our desire to visit Tuva; the officer knew where it
was. (A stamp collector, perhaps?) We told him there was no
Intourist office there; instead of giving us a typical bureaucratic response ("If there's no Intourist office there, then obvi-

---

[6]Two of the five were still alive when our adventure began. Sedip-ool died in 1985;
Kamova died at the end of 1988.

ously you can't go!"), he asked, "Is there some kind of institute in Tuva?"

"Oh, yes!" I exclaimed.

"It's the TNIIYaLI—the Tuvinskii Nauchno-Issledovatel'-
skii Institut Yazyka, Literatury, i Istorii," said Glen, flawlessly
reeling off the tongue twister.

"We have been in contact with one of its members," I
added.

"Well, then," the officer said, "perhaps you could ask the
institute to send a letter of invitation . . ."

"That's all?" I asked incredulously. "Just a letter from the
institute?"

"That's all you need."

"Not even anything from Moscow?"

"No, an official letter from the institute in Kyzyl addressed
to us is sufficient. When it arrives we will notify you and issue
you a visa."

"That's great. We'll do it! We'll see you in a couple of
months!"

We shook hands with the officer—I felt like hugging him—
and floated out of the consulate. As we got into Glen's car, I
said, "We can't blow this chance. Tuvan is fun to decipher
and dabble in, but it isn't working for us as an effective means
of communication. A letter in Russian will set everything
right. Then the institute will understand exactly what we
need: a letter of invitation addressed to the consulate."

We drove to a Russian bookstore about a mile away. Glen
found a book on how to write business letters in Russian; now
he needed a Russian typewriter. At the bookstore he got some
names of possible sources, but none of them panned out. Out
of desperation we looked in the yellow pages and found a man
named Archie, who had a small shop near Chinatown.
"Come on over," he said. "I'll make you really good deeel!"

Glen got a "deeel" indeed—a Ukrainian typewriter for
$25. It worked fine for Russian, since Ukrainian is written in

the Cyrillic alphabet as well. But hunting for letters on an unfamiliar keyboard proved to be slow, so Glen wrote out the first draft of the letter by hand.

I took the English translation of the letter to Pasadena, showed it to Richard (who said it was fine), and sent it back to Glen. He typed up the Russian version on his new typewriter and sent it off.

Another school year began (again with no geography classes); drumming and storytelling sessions with Feynman continued. We tried to be guarded in our hopes for the latest plan to succeed, but we knew this time it *had* to work.

One day Richard called me up. "Come over here, man, I've got something to show you."

I jogged over to the Feynmans'.

Richard was holding a twelve-inch phonograph record, called *Melodii Tuvy*. It had been delivered by Kip Thorne, a Caltech physicist who worked closely with Braginsky and Ginzburg, the Russian scientists Richard knew. Thorne had just returned from Moscow.

There was a note written in Russian on the back jacket: we could make out our names; the rest turned out to be "With sincere respect and best wishes. With Tuvan greetings, S. Vainshtein." An accompanying message from Professor Thorne said, "Letter from Vainshtein to RPF has been mailed. With help of Director of Institute [of Ethnography in Moscow] he is trying to arrange permission for RPF to visit Tuva."

As euphoria set in, Richard took the record out of its jacket. I went over to the record player, dusted it off, cleaned off the needle, carefully placed the record on the platen, and took a deep breath. When my hand stopped shaking, I placed the needle carefully on the record.

What we heard was so wonderful, I'd like you to hear it for yourself. (A special sound sheet is included with this book. Play it now!)

Hail to the Chief!

4   WE were in shock. Tuva, isolated in the center of Asia—that little lost land of enchanting postage stamps—had transcended our wildest dreams. The sounds on the record were stunning: how could two notes be produced simultaneously by a single singer? At first the higher "voice" sounded like a flute, several octaves higher than the fundamental tone. Then came even stranger styles of *höömei,* the most bizarre of which was the "rattling" style, which sounded like a long-winded frog.

It took several days for us to recover. Finally, I sent the mysterious sounds to all the Friends of Tuva, including Mary Zirin, who suggested I send a copy to Mario Casetta, the charismatic deejay of ethnic music on KPFK, the local independent radio station.

To Mr. Casetta, I simply wrote, "Guess what this is, and where it comes from—Ralph Leighton, 577-<u>8882</u>." (The hint was to see which letters on the telephone correspond to 8882.)

Casetta responded right away. "It sounds like something I have on a record from Mongolia," he said enthusiastically. (Indeed, his record contained some *höömei* from western Mongolia, where several thousand Tuvans live.)

I told him the mysterious sounds were from the land once known as Tannu Tuva.

"Tannu Tuva—you mean the place with those beautiful postage stamps?" (Mario, too, had collected Tuva's distinctive stamps as a boy.) "We'll have to do a show—just give me some time to rummage around the attic and find my collection."

At the end of October Richard had some medical tests done at UCLA. The results were "interesting" from Richard's point of view; they were disastrous from everyone else's perspective: the cancer in his abdomen that supposedly had been removed three years before had now spread in a complicated pattern around his intestines.

Dr. Donald Morton of UCLA's John Wayne Cancer Clinic was called in to operate. "I believe in cutting away an inch of good tissue around every place I find cancer," said the surgeon. "I usually don't stop until I can see the operating table underneath."

"What are the odds in an operation like that?" Richard asked.

"Well, I've had a dozen patients, and I haven't lost one yet—but I still don't know what my limitations are."

Richard took radiation therapy to soften up the cancerous tissue, and then underwent what was to be a ten-hour operation. As he was being sewn up, an artery close to his heart burst. He required eighty pints of blood before it was over. Coincidentally, there had been two other patients at UCLA with similar needs that day, so the blood bank was running

dry. An alert went out to Caltech and its affiliate, the Jet
Propulsion Laboratory. Within two hours there was a line of a
hundred volunteers from Pasadena donating blood into the
"bank account" of Richard Feynman.

The surgery ended up taking fourteen hours. His recovery
was slow, but Richard didn't complain—he was already living
on borrowed time.

In December a colorful envelope appeared in my mailbox—an early Christmas card, perhaps? I soon realized what
it was: Daryma had replied, at last! I took it over to Richard
and we opened the envelope together. An entertaining week
of deciphering ensued, with the following results:

> Greetings, friends Ralph Leighton and Richard!
>
> How living, working are you? You-with new what is? Us-by
> fall fallen-has. Your sent letters-your received have I. Sent gift
> also received I. Big-with [thanks] full-am-I.
>
> You-to *kargyraa, höömei, sygyt* to-send pledge but found-not
> have I. Found having after send-shall I. [Apparently *Melodii
> Tuvy* was hard to find in Tuva.]
>
> I this year vacation Mongolia-to went-I. Interesting was.
>
> You Russian-Tuvan dictionary found you and translate,
> very good.
>
> You-to what necessary, write you.
>
> Health-happiness have-to-you wish-I.
>
> Big-with [thanks] full-am-I.
>
> Me-knowing friends-your-to greetings-my fill-you.

We sent our translation of Ondar's letter, together with
the one from twenty-two months before, to Professor Krueger
to check their accuracy. Krueger wrote back, "The style is
obviously very direct and simple, and with your permission, I
shall make use of both of them for instructional purposes.
The students ought to be able to read them rather soon."
Apparently these letters were child's play for students of Turkic languages.

We wrote a short letter to Ondar wishing him a Happy New Year, introduced him to Glen Cowan, and asked whether his institute had received Glen's letter. We said the weather in Pasadena was "10 degrees of heat" (50 degrees Fahrenheit), and asked what the weather was in Kyzyl (perhaps "10 degrees of cold," or 14 degrees Fahrenheit?). We ended our letter in the customary fashion: "Big-with [thanks] full-are-we."

In January 1982 we received a New Year's greeting from Sevyan Vainshtein. It said, "May your dream of reaching Tuva be realized in the coming year." We took those words to be a sign that he and the director of the Institute of Ethnography in Moscow had made progress in arranging our trip. We began to fantasize about playing drums at the drama theater in Kyzyl.

We also began to prepare for a more immediate program, the yearly Caltech musical. This time it was *South Pacific*. Richard and I were supposed to help set the tone for the mythical island of Bali Hai in a special scene created by the director of Caltech's production, Shirley Marneus. We would be drumming for a quartet of grass skirts slung low on shapely hips that moved like Maytag washers gone haywire.

I had a recording of Tahitian drumming, but all the rhythms except one—a funeral dirge—were so fast, there was no hope for us. So I called up Mario Casetta at KPFK to see if he had some others.

"The man you want to see is Jack Kineer," he said.

Mr. Kineer had a Tahitian drumming group—composed mainly of white suburbanites—that was preparing for a Polynesian dance festival on the "island" of Carson (a city in Los Angeles County with a large Samoan population). He invited Richard and me to attend a rehearsal at his home.

As we walked down the driveway, we followed the pulse of throbbing drums to the garage, and opened a side door. A tidal wave of *tiki-tiki taka-taka toona-taka tiki-taka* plastered us to the wall and assaulted our bodies from head to toe. "You can find *everything* in Los Angeles," Richard cried. "The world is wonderful!"

During a break we talked to Mr. Kineer about Tahiti. It turned out he could speak the language, so Richard learned how to say "Bring on the drummers!" and "Bring on the dancers!" in contemporary Tahitian.

As we drove home, Richard burst out laughing. "The only one in the audience who will understand my Tahitian—besides Tahitians—will be Murray Gell-Mann," he chuckled.

I knew that whether Gell-Mann was in the audience or not, Richard always wanted to be as authentic as possible in the roles he played. For our San Francisco performance of *The Ivory Merchant,* he had learned some phrases in Ewe, a West African language, from Caltech's Africa specialist, Ned Munger.

In early February I was awakened one morning by a thunderstorm. I switched on the radio and drifted in and out of sleep. I began to dream about a guy explaining on the radio how *höömei* worked: "Harmonics are produced in the mouth the same way as with a Jew's harp, but in this case the voice supplies the fundamental tone." Then he proceeded to demonstrate the technique. The strange sounds I had heard until then only on *Melodii Tuvy* were being produced by an American!

My dream continued as the guy on the radio told a story about the origin of *höömei:* "It is said to have begun with a monk hearing overtones produced by a waterfall in a particularly acoustic canyon in Western Mongolia. . . ." I began to wake up—this story was too bizarre even for a dream! I listened to the rain outside, augmented by sounds on the radio of falling water and—I couldn't believe it—*höömei!* The reporter signed off: "This is Tom Vitale in New York."

I staggered around my apartment searching for pen and paper, chanting "Tom Vitale, Tom Vitale, Tom Vitale." I was desperate to know how much of my strange dream had been real. Half an hour later, Mary Zirin called. "Did you hear the report on NPR?"

"I think so," I replied. "Was it really a guy explaining and demonstrating *höömei?*"

"Yes," she said. "The program repeats every two hours, so I'll record it for you when it comes around again just before nine o'clock."

After school I went over to Mary's and listened to the tape of Tom Vitale's report. The guy explaining the singing, David Hykes, had a group in New York called the Harmonic Choir, which usually performed in cathedrals. "What a crazy country we have," I thought.[1] "I have to meet this guy."

I contacted Hykes through NPR, and told him about the efforts of Richard, Glen, and me to reach Tuva. He responded, "There's a guy named Ted Levin who has been trying to get to Tuva for years. I'll give him your phone number."

Levin said there was going to be a *höömei* conference that summer in Hovd, Mongolia. I told Richard about it, and we pulled out an atlas. Hovd (formerly Kobdo), nestled in the Altai Mountains, was only two hundred miles south of Tuva, and connected by road. Presumably, a large contingent of Tuvans would show up for the conference, so we might be able to meet our friend Ondar Daryma there. If we couldn't stow away on the bus taking the Tuvans back to Kyzyl, we could don shepherd's clothes and sneak into Tuva on foot!

I telephoned Professor Krueger in Indiana and told him about the conference. A specialist in Mongolian, he was quite keen to go. He said he would check it out with his contacts in Ulaan Bator.

---

[1] I was too provincial in my thinking. There are harmonic choirs (overtone choirs) in England, France, and Germany as well. Hykes and his Harmonic Choir have produced a number of records, tapes, and CDs of their work, one of which eventually found its way into the sound track for the feature film *Dead Poets Society*.

Our conversation drifted to Otto Mänchen-Helfen. "I met him in Berkeley once," Krueger said. "He was a professor of art history there. He's dead now, but perhaps his wife still lives in the Bay Area."

I told Glen, who began checking around various departments at Berkeley. After a few days he found Guitty Azarpay, a professor of Near Eastern Studies, who had been Mänchen-Helfen's graduate student. "Yes, Dr. Anna Maenchen is still alive, and still has her psychoanalysis practice in Berkeley," she said. Glen made contact with Dr. Maenchen by phone, and arranged for us both to meet her.

She was an extraordinary woman: born in St. Petersburg, she witnessed the Russian Revolution as a teenager. She fled with her family to Germany soon after the Bolsheviks came to power.

Anna met Otto in Berlin. An outspoken Social Democrat, he was forced by the Nazis to leave that city in the early 1930s. After several years in Vienna, where she learned psychoanalysis, they had to flee the Nazis again, and came to the United States.

Dr. Maenchen had her own story to tell about Tuva:

> During the summer of 1929 I was at the resort of Rodaun, near Vienna, and on July 26, my husband's birthday, I tried to send him a telegram. I addressed it to "the town of Kyzyl-Khoto in the country of Tannu Tuva." The postmaster, looking at me as if I were suffering from some sort of mental disease, went to the back of the little post office to look in his books. When he returned, he said triumphantly, "There is no such town of Kyzyl-Khoto, and no such country of Tannu Tuva." I was stubborn, and asked him to send my telegram from the main post office in Vienna. The next day a telegram from Vienna said, "There is no such town; there is no such country." The postmaster was happy to be proven right. Nevertheless, I asked him to include in the address "via Novosibirsk," a Siberian city northwest of Mongolia.

Two months later my husband's expedition, on their Mongolian horses, met a camel caravan. Since such encounters did not happen every day in those steppes inhabited by nomads, both groups stopped, and my husband got the telegram. Not one word was legible, but the date was there, so he knew it was a birthday greeting.[2]

The other reason I had come to San Francisco was to celebrate the Chinese New Year with the family of my girlfriend, Phoebe Kwan. I recalled reading that the Tuvans also observed the Lunar New Year, so I said to Glen, "Hey, let's call up Ondar tonight and wish him Happy *Shagaa.*"

"You're nuts, Ralph."

"I know, but I'll pay for the call. I want to read Ondar some phrases in Tuvan. Will you talk to him in Russian?"

"All right, if you insist."

From Glen's apartment I dialed 00 to reach the overseas operator, who turned out to be in Pittsburgh. There were two ways to call the USSR: one was to wait in a queue and have the operator call us when our turn came up (a three- to nine-hour wait); the other was to make a reservation twenty-three hours in advance. I made a reservation for 10 P.M. the following night, when it would be 1 or 2 P.M. in Kyzyl.

When the time came, I went over to Glen's apartment. An hour later the telephone rang—it was the overseas operator. Glen handled the call.

"What city, please," says the operator.

"Kyzyl."

"Please spell that, sir."

"K-Y-Z-Y-L."

"One moment please."

There were several clicks, a period of silence, and then a voice in Russian—it was the operator in Moscow.

[2]This is part of Dr. Maenchen's foreword to Alan Leighton's translation of *Reise ins asiatische Tuwa.* (See Footnote 2 on page 26.)

"America calling," the overseas operator said. "We would like to call Kyzyl."

"*Which* city?"

"Kyzyl . . ."

Glen said, "Kyzyl, Tuvinskaya ASSR . . ."

"Ah—da, da. Kyzyl."

Some more clicks, more silence, and then a fainter voice came on the line—it was the operator in Kyzyl.

Glen said in Russian, "We wish to speak to the Institute of Language, Literature, and History, the TNIIYaLI."

More silence.

Then came the sound of a telephone ringing. Someone answered.

Glen says, "Allo, eto Glen Cowan. Ya zvonyu iz Kalifornii."

When the person on the other end replied, Glen gestured at the phone and mouthed, "It's Ondar!"

As the conversation continued, my mind's eye could see Ondar sitting in a room a quarter of the way around the world, its floor parallel to our walls. I imagined the route that Glen's voice might be taking to reach Kyzyl: overland from Oakland to Pittsburgh; up to a satellite and back down to Helsinki (where the "hot line" goes); along several hundred miles of telephone line to Moscow; then more than three thousand miles of line over the Urals and across Siberia to Novosibirsk, Abakan, and finally Kyzyl—all in less than half a second!

Glen wished Ondar Happy *Shagaa,* and said that the holiday was celebrated in San Francisco with a big parade through Chinatown. "How is *Shagaa* celebrated in Tuva?" he asked.

"We simply observe it," Ondar replied.

Moving right along, Glen asked about the invitation we had been seeking from Ondar's institute—apparently his masterpiece letter, typewritten in Russian, hadn't arrived. He dictated the address of the Soviet consulate to Ondar, and assured our prospective host that we would pay our own expenses in Tuva, of course.

Ondar said he would take the information to the director of the TNIIYaLI.

Then it was my turn to speak. I began reading from my Tuvan-Mongolian-Russian (and now -English) phrasebook. "Ekii!" (Hello!)

Ondar answered, "Ekii!"

"Baiyrlal-bile xolbashttyr silerge baiyr chedirip tur men!" (I congratulate you with the holiday!)

"Huh-huh . . ."

"Silerning kadyyngar deesh ob dashkany ködürein!" (Lift this toast to your health!)

"Huh-huh . . ."

I went through a half-dozen phrases like that; Ondar answered the same way: "Huh-huh . . ."

I finally ended up with "Baiyrlig!" (Goodbye!)

Ondar answered, "Baiyrlig!"

Oh, well, I thought to myself. At least I can say "hello" and "goodbye" in Tuvan. All the other stuff Ondar didn't seem to understand, so I'll have to stick to single words when I talk to the Tuvans in Tuva.

When I got back to Pasadena, rehearsals for *South Pacific* were in full swing. For Richard the students had fashioned a tall headdress with colorful feathers accompanied by a long cape festooned with seashells. I was assigned a loincloth. The director kept referring to Richard as "the Chief," and I began doing it, too.

On opening night the Chief was still short on endurance— he had to sleep during most of the performance, getting up only for the Bali Hai scene. But when he commanded the drummers and dancers—in Tahitian—to join him on stage, his voice was strong and confident. He drummed for only a few minutes, but with such gusto that he looked as if he had recovered one hundred percent. It was his first appearance in

"The Chief of Bali Hai" beats out a frenzied rhythm for an appreciative Caltech audience. (Courtesy California Institute of Technology.)

public since that harrowing fourteen-hour operation three months before, so it was an emotional moment for the audience—especially for the army of volunteers, who were obviously satisfied that their blood had been put to good use. Our scene stopped the show, to deafening applause and a standing ovation.

We Appear in the Center of Asia

5 AT the end of February I got a call from Mario Casetta at KPFK: he had found his stamp collection. I took *Melodii Tuvy* and some tapes of the Harmonic Choir over to the radio station to record the Tuva show, during which Mario appointed himself director of the Silverlake[1] chapter of the Friends of Tuva. After the show was broadcast, interest in membership trickled in from KPFK's listeners. Each time Mario repeated the show (about once a year), I would receive greetings from fellow Tuva enthusiasts at 246-TUVA, my telephone number at the time.

Getting that number took some sneakiness on my part—and some goodwill on the part of the telephone company. I first got the idea of having a special number when I got the palin-

---

[1]Silverlake is an artsy district of Los Angeles, northeast of Hollywood, where Mario lives.

drome 798-8897 purely by chance. When I moved to another address, I asked the telephone company which prefixes were available. I then tried each prefix followed by the numbers -8882. 577-8882 gave me a recording that said, "The number you have dialed is not in service at this time." That was what I was looking for: 577-TUVA was available.

The customer service representative fixed me up with no problem.

A few years later, when I moved to a nearby town that had different prefixes, there were new regulations: special phone numbers that made words now cost extra—there was a market for this kind of thing among certain businesses, as in "FOR-CARS" and the like—so you had to show that the word had something to do with your name if you didn't want to pay a fee.

I said, "I'd like my number listed under Tuva—Tannu Tuva."

The service rep says, "Is Tuva the last name?"

"Yes. And Tannu is the first name."

The plan worked; I got 246-8882. When I told Richard the number, he said, "8882 spells TUVA; maybe 246 spells something, too." (It does.)

When the new telephone book came out there was a listing for "Tannu Tuva", who soon received all sorts of sophisticated junk mail—including an invitation to buy season tickets to the Los Angeles Philharmonic Orchestra.

Another Tuva convert—a fellow teacher in Pasadena—happened to have 8882 already as the last four digits of his telephone number. When he realized they spelled TUVA, he said, "Wow! That's great! Until now I thought the best thing about those numbers was the famous tune you get when you play them on a touch-tone phone!"

Sometime in March I got a call from Professor Krueger. "There has been a purge of the Mongolian Politburo," he said. "The Minister of Culture has been replaced. The *höömei* conference has been canceled."

That was a real blow to our fantasies. Of all the ways we had cooked up to get to Tuva, the Mongolian route would have been by far the most exciting. With Glen's letter to Ondar's institute apparently falling into a crack (or an FBI file) somewhere, our most realistic chance of reaching Tuva now rested with the director of Vainshtein's institute in Moscow.

In April of 1982, Argentina invaded a remote, isolated land on the opposite side of the world from Tuva—the Falkland Islands. Meanwhile, all spring long, we heard neither from Kyzyl nor from Moscow about our coveted invitations. Two months later, as the Falklands war was ending, another war intensified: Israel invaded southern Lebanon.

Depressed by the state of affairs in the world, I invited the Chief on a whim to celebrate his sixty-fourth birthday a month late in Las Vegas. We found a place just off the strip where the hotels he knew—the Flamingo, El Rancho, and the Tropicana—were located.

Upon our arrival we were each given a "funbook" full of coupons to make bets with at various tables. We calculated that each book was worth $17.50, nearly the cost of our room. We went downstairs and used all the coupons (but made no further bets) and netted about $50. Richard said, "This is the way to gamble, man—when the odds are in your favor!"

We proceeded to take in a show (on a coupon, of course), which featured a comedian called "Mundane the Grate," whose act was full of plays on words. We were in hysterics.

Two days later, as we were checking out of our hotel, the desk clerk said, "How would you like your two-dollar room key deposit paid back—in cash, or in chips?"

"How about in funbooks?" I said.

To our surprise and delight, the guy handed us four funbooks and kept the $2. We immediately went over to a craps table and put down two coupons.

After we collected our winnings from the first table, we proceeded to another craps table to use another two coupons. But before we could place our bets, a man in a suit came over and whispered something to a large man with no neck who was sitting between the two croupiers, guarding the chips. Mr. No-Neck said, "Gentlemen, you will have to leave the table."

We protested that we had obtained the four funbooks in good faith, but seeing the look in Mr. No-Neck's eyes, we decided not to push our luck—at least not at craps. We proceeded quickly to the 21 table and made a single bet, and then rushed over to the "wheel of fortune" before making our exit.

We hadn't used up all our coupons, but at least I could proudly boast to my friends that we had been sent away from the tables in Las Vegas for winning too much.

Back in Pasadena there was a letter waiting for me. Glen had found some interesting information in Russian[2] about the mysterious English traveler in Mänchen-Helfen's book. According to Glen's translation, it said:

Take a look at a map of Asia—the largest of the continents. Between its outermost points on each edge, draw two straight lines—from the north to the south and from the east to the west. These lines will intersect on the territory of a small mountain country lying in a deep hollow at the upper reaches of the mighty Siberian river Yenisei. This country, situated in the very center of Asia, equally far from the icy expanses of the Arctic and from the warm Indian Ocean, from the ancient Ural Mountains and from the azure immensity of the waters of the Pacific, is called Tuva.

In the previous century, Tuva was visited by a certain trav-

[2]In Yuri Promptov, *V Tsentre Aziatskogo Materika (In the Center of the Asian Continent)* (Moscow, 1950).

eler, moved by a feeling of sporting excitement. Before this he had succeeded in being in the center of two continents— Europe and Africa. The traveler got the urge to go to the center of great Asia. With great difficulty, in conditions of complete "roadlessness," he made his way through the Siberian taiga, crossed the Sayan Mountains, and finally got to the headwaters of the Yenisei. By means of complicated calculations he had precisely established on the map the point to which he was headed, and on a terrace of a steppe over the blue Yenisei he erected a wooden column with the inscription "Centre of Asia." Having reached his goal and having established this distinctive geographical record, the traveler set out on his return journey, not making any attempt to further acquaint himself with the difficult-to-reach country which he had gotten into.

This was essentially the same story recited by Mänchen-Helfen, with minor discrepancies—a wooden column versus a stone monument, and Europe versus North and South America for the continents whose centers had already been reached. Then Alan reported finding a source from 1927 with a similar story.[3] I decided to research the matter during summer vacation. Who was this eccentric English traveler?

Three years before, as part of my general research on Tuva, I had written to the Royal Geographical Society in London and told them the story as related by Otto Mänchen-Helfen. I received a reply from Mr. G. S. Dugdale, librarian at the Royal Geographic Society. He wrote:

> We have a copy of *Reise ins asiatische Tuwa* and I was interested to find the passage to which you refer. . . . I have been answering geographical inquiries in this Library for over 20

[3]Nikolai I. Leonov, *Tannu Tuva: Strana goluboi reki (Tannu Tuva: Land of the Light-Blue River)* (Moscow, 1927).

years but have never been asked about this unidentified English world traveler. I only wish we could discover something about this. . . .

At UCLA I stumbled upon *Whitaker's Almanac,* published in London during the late nineteenth and early twentieth centuries, during the heyday of exploration by European travelers of every stripe to every corner of the world. I checked every year from 1881 (the first year UCLA had) through 1900. The section on Asia for 1885 was typical. It read:

ASIA still finds occupation for numerous explorers. Dr. Sven Hedin, who returned to Kashgar in October last year, after having spent four months on the Mustagh Ata, started again on February 17, with the intention of going to Tibet. On crossing the sandy desert of Takla Makan he nearly perished of thirst. Two of his men and six camels died, most of his outfit was lost, and he was compelled to return to Kashgar. Fortunately he was able to save his maps and journals. Mr. and Mrs. Littledale were more fortunate. They started in November, 1884, on a second journey to Central Asia, and are reported to have reached Kashmir a year afterwards, having succeeded in crossing Western Tibet. Prince Henry of Orleans, who has already crossed Asia from west to east, is now engaged upon a similar journey in the opposite direction. He is accompanied by MM. Briffand and Roux. Since February last he has traveled along the northern frontier of Tonking as far as the Mekhong river, he then turned north, and on May 25 reached Talifu, in Yunnan. The exploration of the Tien Shan was completed last year by M. Obruchev. Another Russian explorer, M. Roborovsky, having confirmed, by careful observation, the surprisingly low altitude (−360 ft.) of the Turfan basin, in the very heart of Central Asia, crossed the western Gobi to Sha-chan, and spent part of the present year in an exploration of the mountain regions in the direction of the Kuku Nor. . . .

I could see Phileas Fogg and the other old fogies in their bowler hats sitting around the Reform Club, reading *Whitaker's Almanac* and debating the latest travels of Mr. and Mrs. Littledale in Tibet. I was sure that before I reached 1900 I would find a passage that read, "In the Chinese territory of Urianghai, Mr. Whittlesley has succeeded in erecting another monument to the centre of a continent." But alas, 1900 came and went without revealing the identity of the Englishman who, it seemed, was so eccentric that he didn't even appear in the bible of eccentric explorers.

I then turned to the question of determining the center of Asia.[4] Promptov's description of intersecting lines, whose endpoints were "the outermost points on each edge of Asia," was vague, at best. A more reasonable method was to cut out a map of Asia and balance it on the head of a pin. Could the mysterious English traveler have done that?

I went to the UCLA map library and found several historical maps to copy. When I got home I pasted them to pieces of cardboard and cut them out with the care of a silhouette artist. According to the infamous Mercator projection, by which Greenland looks as big as South America, the "center" of Asia came out northeast of Tuva; the equal area and conic projections put the center far to the southwest. I finally found a map from the 1850s, called "Gall's stereographic projection," that worked: the "center" of Asia was right on the Yenisei River near Kyzyl.

---

[4]To this end, Richard offered several definitions and wrote out a mathematical formula full of cosines and sines for one of them, which I programmed into my little Sinclair ZX81 computer. After inputting the latitude and longitude of several hundred points around the perimeter of Asia, I found that the center of Asia according to this formula was 45° 31' North and 86° 59' East, in the middle of some sand dunes in the Dzungarian Basin—about 115 miles north of Ürümchi (and only 50 miles east of what I had determined to be the point farthest from any ocean), but more than 500 miles southwest of Kyzyl.

Of course I couldn't say that the mysterious Englishman had used this method until I found another example, so I pasted the Gall's stereographic projection of North America to a piece of cardboard, cut it out, and balanced it on the head of a pin. The geographical center came out to be in southern Saskatchewan—to the north of Rugby, North Dakota, where a monument marks the spot today.

At the UCLA library I found a book called *Saskatchewan Monuments*—I could hardly believe my luck—but alas, none of them marked the center of North America. Undaunted, I telephoned several libraries in Saskatchewan, including the major ones in Saskatoon, Regina, and Moosejaw. One of them had a local history desk, staffed by Julie Harris and Brock Silversides.

Ms. Harris took my call. After I explained the whole story, she said, "I recall there was a small town near here that once claimed to be the geographical center of North America, but no longer does."

"That's perfect!"

But after a few weeks, Ms. Harris still could not locate the town. The subject remains a mystery.

As fall approached there was still no word from Moscow or Kyzyl, but there was nothing we could do—we couldn't exactly write to Vainshtein and Daryma and say, "Hey, what about our invitations!"

In October, the Polish parliament outlawed the independent trade union Solidarity. I followed the example of President Reagan and placed a candle in my window as a symbol of hope for freedom in Poland. I didn't dare imagine that in less than seven years, Solidarity would emerge to form the first non-Communist government in Eastern Europe. But the first step in that process would happen one month later.

One morning in November, Glen called me up. "Lenny Brezhnev is dead," he said. "I switched on my shortwave radio late last night to Radio Magadan, but instead of the regular program, there was marshal music. Every hour an announcer would come on and say . . ."

Glen turned on his tape recording of the broadcast and translated:

> Attention, attention comrades! The Central Committee of the Communist Party of the Soviet Union, the Presidium of the Supreme Soviet of the Union of Soviet Socialist Republics and the Council of Ministers of the USSR, with deep grief, inform the Party and the entire Soviet people that on November 10, 1982, at 8:30 A.M., after a long illness, the General Secretary of the Central Committee of the Communist Party of the Soviet Union and Chairman of the Presidium of the Supreme Soviet of the Union of Soviet Socialist Republics, Leonid Ilyich Brezhnev, an outstanding figure of the Communist Party and Soviet government and steadfast soldier for the ideals of communism and for peace, passed away. He will live forever in the hearts of the Soviet people and of all progressive mankind.

The local stations in Los Angeles were just beginning to broadcast the news: Leonid Brezhnev, the man with the big bushy eyebrows who engineered the ouster of Nikita Khrushchev eighteen years before, was gone. He was succeeded a few days later by KGB chief Yuri Andropov.

Later that month I was invited to go with Richard to the Esalen Institute, a "secular monastery" on the California coast south of Monterey. He was to conduct a week-long seminar called "The Quantum Mechanical View of Reality" for people wary of "establishment science." My job was to teach them drumming as an antidote to the "heavy thinking" that would be required for the physics part.

As we drove up the coast I kept stopping to take pictures. The Chief became more and more impatient to reach our destination. When we arrived, I understood why: there is no more beautiful place on the California coast than Esalen—especially when one takes into account the added attraction of nudes sunning themselves on massage tables, or soaking in baths fed by natural hot springs perched on a cliff.

At the end of the week, after completing his seminar on quantum mechanics,[5] Richard said he felt out of place.

"I know what you mean," I said. "In the bookstore there are books on yoga, gestalt, pyramid power, something called 'Rolfing,' and even one called *Sex and the Brain*. Right in the middle of all that mush is *The Character of Physical Law* by R. P. Feynman."[6]

"Yeah. Next time, I want to do something different."

"Well," I said, "those stories you've been telling me when we drum together—there's a certain aspect about them that almost amounts to a philosophy of sorts. We just need to think of a word for it."

Richard listed topics while I took notes and toyed with possible titles. Faustin Bray, the imaginative force behind the Chief's Esalen experiences, added the proper buzzwords to make the description acceptable for the Esalen catalog. When she was finished, it said:

Idiosyncratic Thinking

The aim of the week is to help participants develop a unique personal philosophy which can bring peace of mind and enjoyment of life's contradictions.

In science, when we look at common things from some new and unexpected viewpoint, we achieve a new and deeper understanding. When this same approach is applied to personal problems,

[5] Some of the material appeared in his subsequent book, *QED: The Strange Theory of Light and Matter* (Princeton University Press, 1985; paperback edition, 1989).
[6] MIT Press, © 1965; tenth printing 1982.

useful unexpected insights are often realized. This concept will be illustrated in two ways: through discussions of personal human ideas such as doubt, uncertainty, remorse, guilt, responsibility, dignity, and freedom; and by looking at nature as a teacher with these ideas in mind. Participants are invited to contribute their thoughts for discussion in the sessions.

The thinking and experiencing process will be integrated using a blend of esoteric skills, music, visual arts, and fun. You are invited to bring rhythm instruments.

As the New Year approached I shopped for greeting cards to send Vainshtein and Daryma. When Glen visited Pasadena for the Christmas holidays, I showed him the card I had picked out: the scene was a log cabin in the snow, with a pair of wheel tracks leading to it.

Glen looked at it in horror. "Ralph, we can't send that card. It looks cute and quaint to us because scenes like that are several generations in our past. But to a Soviet, it might be an all-too-real reminder of how underdeveloped life is today in Siberia."

"No kidding?"

"No kidding."

We ended up sending cards showing Santa riding a surfboard.

While Glen was in town he proposed a plan. "Let's take a picture of ourselves, and send it to *Tuvinskaya Pravda.* I bet I can get it printed."

"It can't hurt," I said. "Maybe Ondar's institute will pay more attention to us if we've been in Kyzyl's newspaper. But what makes you think you can get it printed?"

Glen reminded me that he subscribed to *Pravda,* which was sent every day by express mail from Moscow to his apartment in Oakland for only 50¢ a week—obviously a heavily subsidized price. "I figure every ruble they spend on delivering *Pravda* to me is one less ruble spent on defense," he said.

"The stuff is so predictable, it's a joke!" He cited an example: " 'A reader from Kavalerovo Village in the Primorskii Region writes, "I read that in China a new five-year plan of economic development has been accepted. Tell about it.' "—Gimme a break!"

Since the Tuvan New Year was coming up, Glen suggested we send *Shagaa* greetings with our photo. I got Yasushi Ohnuki (the Kurosawa fan who took me to see *Dersu Uzala*) and his son Tohru to take pictures of the Chief, Glen, and me. Richard had the idea of pushing my car with great effort to show how hard we were working to get to Tuva. Yasushi snapped the picture as Richard joked, "We should call this one 'Tuva or Bust!' "

Glen advised us that the editors of *Tuvinskaya Pravda* wouldn't have the sense of humor to accept such a photo. So we sent a picture of the three of us standing next to my car, with the TOUVA license plate clearly visible. Glen wrote a little article in Russian that said:

Happy *Shagaa!* We, residents of California Ralph Leighton, Dr. Richard Feynman, and Glen Cowan, would like, through your newspaper, to wish the people of the Tuvinskaya ASSR a heart-felt greeting.

We are amazed by the beauty, the richness and variety of nature in your republic, located in the heart of Asia. We are especially interested in Tuvan ethnography and music. We listen with great interest to a recording of Tuvan folk music styles "sygyt," "kargyraa," and "höömei," which we received as a gift from Dr. S. I. Vainshtein of the Miklukho-Maklay Institute of Ethnography in Moscow.

We believe that today, when our planet is going through such a difficult time, it is very important to express our wishes for good relations, as well as peace and friendship between our peoples. We wish you happiness, good health, and success.

With sincere respect and greetings from California, [and then our signatures].

"Tuva or Bust!" Richard struggles to push Ralph's car a few feet along the road to Tuva. (Courtesy Yasushi Ohnuki.)

Despite Glen's impressive capabilities in Russian, I didn't have much hope that our faces would appear in Kyzyl. I had already written to *Tuvinskaya Pravda* a few years earlier, requesting a copy of their Tuvan edition. I had even enclosed some International Reply Coupons so it wouldn't cost the Tuvans anything to send it, but I got nothing.

Soon after we sent our *Shagaa* greetings to *Tuvinskaya Pravda*, we received New Year's greetings from Sevyan Vainshtein—but no word on whether he and the director of his institute in Moscow had succeeded in arranging our trip to Tuva.

In the spring of 1983 a reusable "space shuttle" named *Challenger* made its maiden voyage. Meanwhile, Glen flew to New York to be interviewed by an organization called International Research and Exchange (IREX), in the hope of spending a year in the Soviet Union as a physics graduate student. He was the perfect candidate, knowledgeable in his subject and fluent in Russian as well. He passed with flying colors. He would go to Moscow in the fall, after the Soviet Ministry of Higher Education found him a place to study.

This opened up our best chance yet of reaching our goal: soon the Friends of Tuva would have one of their charter members on location in Moscow! With his quick mind, his great charm, and his excellent knowledge of Russian, Glen would get our trip fixed up with ease. It was only a matter of time now.

Our research on Tuva continued. In May Alan sent away to the U.S. government for a listing of Landsat photos from 49° to 54° North and from 88° to 99° East. A few weeks later I received a twenty-page computer printout listing hundreds of photos—it showed their location, types of filters used, percentage of cloud cover, date of acquisition, and overall quality. The catalog said that a single photo (10 inches square) could be obtained for less than $100. I ordered one listed as having no cloud cover, with Kyzyl near its center.

When I received the Landsat photo in the mail, I took it over to the Feynmans'. Richard pulled out a large magnifying glass from his desk and we studied the photograph inch by inch. It clearly showed the two branches of the Yenisei River merging into what the Tuvans call the "Ulug Khem," or "Big River." The wooded Sayan Mountains to the north of Kyzyl were dark, save their snow-capped peaks; the arid steppes to the south and west were light. The thin thread of the Ussinski Trakt, Tuva's main road connection with Siberia, was visible. The bowl around Turan was quite distinct; it and half a dozen other places around Tuva had some mysterious hatchmarks. We theorized that they might be big collective farms.

I framed the photograph and hung it on the wall of my 10 by 12-foot "living room," across from the big Defense Mapping Agency navigation chart of Tuva, which I had mounted on Masonite.

In June, as the space shuttle *Challenger* made its second flight, Sally Ride made history as the first American woman in space.

A month later a schoolgirl from Maine named Samantha Smith, who had written a letter to Yuri Andropov asking him not to start a nuclear war, also made history by attending a Young Pioneer camp on the Black Sea as the personal guest of the Soviet leader.

I discussed this development with Glen. "Maybe I should write to Andropov myself," I said. "Are there any Young Pioneer camps in Tuva?"

"Are you kidding?" he laughed. "It'll never work—you're not as cute as Samantha Smith."

As the summer waned, Korean Airlines flight 007 ended abruptly in the sea. At first the Soviets denied shooting down the airliner. Then they were silent on the matter. A day later Secretary of State Shultz went before the United Nations and played CIA tapes that had a Soviet jet fighter pilot saying, "The target has been hit."

The Soviet Union lost face. Relations between the superpowers soured even more. The IREX participants from the Soviet Union, having just arrived in the United States, were called home out of concern for their safety. The Soviet Ministry of Higher Education had not yet found Glen a place to study.

Despite Glen's earlier ridicule, I wanted to try the Samantha Smith strategy anyway. I proposed writing to each member of the Politburo, including Andropov, appealing to them not to let the KAL tragedy prevent the American IREX participants from going to Moscow. "Just one telephone call from just one Politburo member could solve your problem," I said. "It doesn't cost much to Xerox and post a letter a dozen times."

Glen reluctantly agreed to translate my letter into Russian, and added the proper euphemisms so it would be read sympathetically. But as the weeks went by, it gradually became clear that Glen and the other IREX participants would not be allowed to go to Moscow.

There was one bit of cheerful news that autumn, however; it came from Sevyan Vainshtein. He wrote that he had visited Tuva in June, and was surprised to find an article in *Tuvinskaya Pravda* with greetings from California, accompanied by a particular photograph—he enclosed three copies. Although Glen had failed to reach Moscow, we could now say, thanks to him, that we had appeared in the "Centre of Asia."

Three Americans
Reach Tuva

6 SHORTLY after we got the kick of seeing ourselves in *Tuvinskaya Pravda*, my brother sent me September's European edition of *Geo*. There was an article called "Sibirien—der Riese hinter Europa" ("Siberia—The Giant Beyond Europe"). I called up Richard and he came over.

We turned to the first page of the article. It was a photograph—an aerial shot spread across two pages—of a series of hills covered with short, yellow-green grass. On the left was a small herd of yaks—most were black, some were white—tended by two men on horseback. On the right a hundred sheep were crowded into a corral. There were two yurts, both white with brown tops: the one in the background stood next to a hitching post; the one in the foreground had a small white automobile parked nearby. Several cows lazed about, along with a pig or two. It was an *aal*—a nomad's camp.

This was the first color photograph of Tuva we had ever seen.

Once again, my high school German was put to practical use. The caption was entitled, "A land with a thousand faces." It said:

> Between the Urals, the border of Europe, and the distant Pacific Ocean lies nothing but Siberia—a colossal landmass with permafrost in the north, fire-spewing volcanoes on Kamchatka, oil prospecting in the tundra, the world's largest hydro-electric power station at Shushenskoye, and unspoiled nature in the taiga. Right in the middle of the Asian continent, at the headwaters of the Yenisei and the border of Mongolia, the Siberia of the nomadic Tuvans appears to be as isolated from the rest of the world as a pioneer outpost in America's Wild West. In the high mountains the Tuvans herd yaks. The nomads have a highly developed milking economy with a byproduct loved all over the Soviet Union: from milk they make vodka.[1]

Among the two dozen photos of Siberia, there were three other color photographs of Tuva. They revealed that the heads of small Tuvan children are shaved except for one lock of hair at the front, that the hair color of one Tuvan girl can carry both very dark and very light shades of brown, and that Tuvan fields are plowed in a striped pattern of alternating five-meter-wide swaths.

The pattern reminded Richard of the Landsat photo. We carefully inspected the areas with hatchmarks under a magnifying glass. Sure enough, one of them was right where the Geo photo had been taken.

The text of the article, written by a Russian, emphasized the great industrial progress of Siberia. Nevertheless, that sin-

[1] That was a reference to arak, the mildly intoxicating brew made from fermented mares' milk, developed by the nomads of Eurasia over the centuries.

gle photograph spread over two pages showing yaks and yurts heralded the news that postage-stamp Tuva was still alive in 1983.

As Christmas approached I hit upon a gift idea at a shopping mall: an entrepreneur was offering custom jigsaw puzzles made from any photograph. I rushed home to find the Xerox copy of a certain photo I had found in a Los Angeles library. A week later the other Friends of Tuva were piecing together likenesses of the holy shrine of eccentric travelers, the "Centre of Asia" monument in Kyzyl.

In January 1984 an envelope from the Soviet consulate in San Francisco appeared in my mailbox. Had Ondar's institute sent a letter of invitation with our names to the consulate, as Glen had requested over the phone? That would be a miracle!

The cover letter said:

Dear Mr. Leighton:

It is my pleasure to forward to you a response to your letter from V. V. Grishin, member of the Politburo of the Central Committee of the Communist Party of the Soviet Union. . . .

Grishin's letter (in Russian) was typed—not Xeroxed, as ours had been—and bore his signature in the blue ink of a fountain pen. I thought to myself, Wow! The Samantha Smith strategy worked after all! The letter looked impressive: there were all sorts of CCCPs all over it. I thought, I'd better phone Glen to pack his bags!

I turned the page and scanned the "unofficial translation" provided by the consulate. It began:

Dear Mr. Leighton:

I have read your letter very attentively and share your concern about the serious deterioration of Soviet-American relations which is accompanied by anti-Soviet campaign led by President Reagan's administration. . . .

Already Mr. Grishin had departed from my thoughts. His letter continued:

> We in the Soviet Union note with great concern a sharp escalation of international tensions. The US plans to deploy new medium-range missiles in Western Europe, which are the first-strike weapons aimed at the USSR, increase the threat to peace. . . .

I hadn't said anything about missiles in my letter. Even though Mr. Grishin's reply was typed on an old mechanical typewriter and signed by the Politburo member himself, it was obviously a form letter. There was no mention of Glen's situation.

In early February Yuri Andropov, who seemed to be leading a cautious movement of reform, died after only fifteen months in power. He was succeeded by one of Brezhnev's old buddies, seventy-two-year-old Konstantin Chernenko.

Later than month, before heading for Esalen to conduct his first seminar on "Idiosyncratic Thinking," Richard went with me to see the Dalai Lama of Tibet at the Pasadena Civic Auditorium. The Dalai Lama spoke with excitement about the wonders of nature as revealed by science. The Chief thoroughly enjoyed the occasion, especially the way the "simple Buddhist monk"—as the Dalai Lama referred to himself—used humor (usually at his own expense) to make a point. The Dalai Lama's approach to life reminded me of a quotation Richard attributed to his mother: "The highest forms of understanding we can achieve are laughter and human compassion."

What an encounter it would be, I thought, if the Chief and the Dalai Lama could meet! But alas, our upcoming seminar at Esalen prevented me from arranging such a tête-à-tête (although I tried, just the same).

The seminar on "Idiosyncratic Thinking" was basically an exercise in learning how to think for yourself. Although the participants started out hanging on his every word, Richard eventually got them to challenge him, and some interesting discussions ensued.

In one session, called "The Proud Parent," the Chief asked whether a parent could justifiably be congratulated for the successes of a good child. For those who answered yes, he then asked whether a parent should therefore accept the blame for the failures of a bad child. He talked about the damage done by "experts," whose pronouncements on child-rearing made parents feel inadequate. "As in education, nobody knows how to do it," counseled the neophyte guru. "Just do the best you can, and don't let someone else's opinions or good fortune make you lose your confidence."

Afterwards, a shy woman who hadn't said much in the discussion came up to the Chief. "I appreciate the remarks you made about parenting," she said. "I adopted a two-year-old boy who was very difficult to raise. When he was sixteen he committed suicide."

While I limited my participation at Esalen to drumming and soaking in the hot pools, Richard immersed himself in a new avocation—massage. By the end of the week he had rubbed his hands up and down the well-oiled bodies of men and women (strongly preferring the latter) of all shapes and sizes. On the night before we were to leave for Pasadena, he burst through the door of our cabin and proudly proclaimed, "Hey, man, I'm a real masseuse!" (The way he pronounced the comical description of himself made it rhyme with "moose.")

Richard proceeded to describe—stroke by stroke—the long, slow massage he had given that evening to a woman he had met in class. He introduced her muscle groups as if they were sections in a symphony orchestra, and described how he progressed from one muscle group to another with increasing intensity until the woman heaved a heavy sigh of relaxation, proclaiming that it was the best massage she had ever had.

Back in the real world, spring brought news of the CIA secretly mining Nicaraguan harbors. The only fiendish plan that blossomed in my brain was related to the year we were in, 1984: October would mark the fortieth anniversary of Tuva's annexation by the Soviet Union. No doubt there would be festivities to celebrate the joyous occasion. Kyzyl certainly would be freshly painted to receive the visiting dignitaries. A parade? Of course—it would pass right in front of the government building in downtown Kyzyl. The grand marshal? Who could be better than the man who had appeared with his two friends in *Tuvinskaya Pravda!* After all, we were undoubtedly celebrities throughout Tuva now.

I wrote a letter to TASS, the Soviet news agency, figuring it would be the most likely organization interested in having someone write about forty years of Soviet Tuva.

As summer approached, I thought about the Olympic Games, set to take place in Los Angeles at the end of July. Tuvans were known for archery, wrestling, and horse riding. I dreamed of discovering a name ending in -ool (the Tuvan form of -son) in the wrestling program, and yelling out "Ekii!" But in May, the USSR and its client states announced they would boycott the Olympic Games.

Nevertheless, I attended the Olympic opening ceremonies. The greatest cheer, besides that for the U.S. team, was raised for the athletes from Romania, which had defied the Soviet boycott of the games. To finish the program a few thousand residents of Southern California marched in, dressed in native costumes from every country that participated in the Olympics, as well as those which did not, including the major republics of the Soviet Union. I thought, There's *got* to be a Tuvan living *somewhere* in Southern California!

The Olympics passed off smoothly. Even the diving boards worked flawlessly, despite a thorough going-over (with shoes on) by me and some friends just two weeks before the opening ceremonies—we performed a comedy diving act for assembled dignitaries from the local Olympic Organizing Committee. (For some reason they chose not to include clown diving as an exhibition sport—at least not in 1984.)

That summer saw virtually no activity relating to Tuva, with nary a word from Moscow or Kyzyl. I completed a master's degree in media and educational technology at California State University, Los Angeles, just in time to go on leave from teaching.

As summer drew to a close, the Chief was visited at Caltech by John Boslough, a writer for the *National Geographic* who was preparing an article about time.

"What's the matter," joked Richard. "Has the *National Geographic* run out of places in the world to write about?"

"Well, not exactly," replied Boslough.

The Chief wasn't interested.[2] "But I'll tell you what," he said. "There's a place in the world that the *National Geographic* still hasn't covered."

"Really?"

Richard began to talk about Tuva.

"It sounds interesting," Boslough said. "Why don't you write me a complete, detailed letter—nine or ten pages—about what you just told me; then write a short letter—one or two pages—and address it to Mr. Grosvenor, president of the National Geographic Society. I attend the meetings where they decide what to write about, and with your detailed letter I'll be able to pitch the idea for you. If Mr. Grosvenor accepts, it'll be easy for you to go to Tuva—the relations between the Society and the USSR are very good."

---

[2]Nevertheless, Boslough's article about time, which finally appeared six years later, began with a reference to Richard Feynman.

When the Chief came over to drum he told me about his meeting with Boslough.

"That's great!" I said with excitement. "It's the best chance we have yet, because it depends mainly on people here in the U.S. rather than people in the USSR."

We decided to work on the long letter first. We would each write a rough draft, and see who expressed what better. Then I would put the paragraphs and phrases together. (I was getting lots of practice by then, as I was writing up several stories that would eventually become part of *Surely You're Joking, Mr. Feynman!*) The whole process would take several weeks, but it didn't matter: we didn't want to blow this opportunity.

After we compared notes I typed up the long letter and brought it to Esalen, where the Chief was playing the role of guru again in his second seminar on "Idiosyncratic Thinking." Glen came down from Berkeley one afternoon and looked over our work—between soaking sessions in the hot pools.

As we relaxed in the serenity of the baths overlooking the ocean, Richard suddenly cried, "Thank you, Dr. Morton!" The Chief never forgot that he was living on borrowed time, and often thanked the man most responsible for it in the same way that others would thank God for giving them another fine day.

At Esalen we talked with kindred spirits about our dream. One of them quoted Arnold Palmer: "The harder I work, the luckier I get." We redoubled our efforts to make our letter to the National Geographic Society irresistible.

Toward the end of the week I rarely saw Richard outside of his seminar. One night, when he returned to our cabin, he said, "I'm going nuts!"

"What do you mean?" I asked.

"I met a girl from Canada who's so beautiful—she looks just like Arlene."

I barely recognized the name of Richard's first wife, who

had died in her twenties. He rarely talked about Arlene, but was obviously still haunted by her memory.[3]

On our way back to Pasadena we took a detour to the countryside around Watsonville and visited Victor and Sara Neher. Victor, a retired Caltech physics professor, was still going strong at eighty: his latest project was investigating some of the physics that goes on in trees—in particular, how the sap gets to the top of a hundred-footer. On chart recorders he measured the daily changes in the trees' thickness and the pressure of the sap inside with equipment he designed and built himself.

"Doesn't the sap rise through capillary action?" I asked.

Dr. Neher smiled. "Capillary action can lift the sap against gravity only a relatively short distance. Even a vacuum at the top of a capillary tube can pull sap up only about thirty-three feet before it breaks up. So, as far as I'm concerned, the search is still on for an answer to this mystery." The Chief was smiling, too—he was always delighted to hear about a topic that the rest of the world was overlooking or taking for granted.

We went indoors for tea. The conversation drifted inevitably to Tuva. The Nehers reminded us of President Eisenhower's observation that people-to-people diplomacy was the most practical way to achieve understanding and peace. Sara showed me the October issue of *Soviet Life* magazine, created as the counterpart to *Life* magazine in a cultural exchange agreement in the 1950s. She and Victor had subscribed to *Soviet Life* from the start. Sara said, "Did you know that Tuva is going to be featured in next month's issue?"

We looked at the preview page. Tuva would be the cover story!

When we returned to Pasadena, I retyped the ten-page let-

---

[3]The story of Arlene, pieced together over ten years, provides the title for *What Do You Care What Other People Think?* (see Footnote 2, p. 8.)

ter to Mr. Boslough that we had honed at Esalen. Then I distilled a shorter version for Mr. Grosvenor, which the Chief okayed, and sent both letters off to the National Geographic Society.

In November, President Reagan was reelected in a landslide over Walter Mondale. The Chief was amazed that Reagan could remain in office after so many scandals that had already surfaced in his administration. "That shows how well I understand people," the part-time Esalen guru said.

When the November issue of *Soviet Life* finally came, I went out to a newsstand that sold foreign papers and bought half a dozen copies for the Friends of Tuva. Richard came over and we pored over the magazine together.

We recognized the cover photo; it had been on the preview page in the Nehers' October issue: it showed a young Tuvan woman wearing a headband that made her look like our idea of an American Indian. On page two was a long article entitled "Tuva: A Republic in the Center of Asia"—five full pages, all in English, of up-to-date information on the country we had had difficulty even finding a picture of a few years before. We read the article slowly, savoring every word:

> Flat steppeland interspersed with low brown hills stretches to the horizon; flocks of sheep graze peacefully here and there. The modern age seems to have passed this unspoiled corner of the world by. Here all is peace and quiet.
>
> The road wound on and on—endlessly. At last we spotted a yurt far ahead. An old shepherd came out to meet us, a smile of welcome on his sunburned face. Like everyone who lives on these boundless steppes, Mongush Chola was the soul of hospitality.

It was exactly our fantasy—to meet a Tuvan standing in front of his yurt.

Chola took part in setting up the republic's first collective farms. He set a remarkable record in 1961: The ewes in his flock produced 170 lambs. During his lifetime he has raised more than 23,000 sheep, and the wool he has sheared would fill several freight cars. His six children also work in agriculture.

Okay, so any shepherd we meet in Tuva turns out to be one of those "hero workers of socialism," carefully selected and placed in our path . . .
Our fantasy returned:

> We sat in front of the shepherd's yurt for a while. When it was time to leave, he sang for us. He sang in what seemed to be two voices at once, one reminiscent of the *homus*, a Tuvinian stringed instrument, and the other the mating call of the woodgrouse at dawn in spring. Since time immemorial the Tuvinians have expressed their innermost feelings with this low-pitched gutteral singing. The shepherd's voice floated over the steppe, filling it with sound. For a moment I felt that I understood the meaning of the ancient Tuvinian song.

There was no photograph of Mongush Chola singing höömei outside of his yurt, but it didn't matter—we could imagine everything clearly. There was, however, a picture of Grigori Shirshin, First Secretary of the Tuvan Communist Party Central Committee. A caption quoted Mr. Shirshin: "What used to be a land of nomad herders and hunters is now an industrial-agrarian republic that contributes more and more each year to the Soviet Union's national economy." On the next two pages were photographs of "industrial-agrarian" Tuva: the giant asbestos mine at Ak-Dovurak, farm machinery in the fields, and the Kyzyl Polytechnic Institute.
The article returned to "our" Tuva, but with a twist:

Nature has many surprises in store for you here. There are saltwater lakes and freshwater lakes, medicinal springs and crystal-clear rivers full of delicious fish. Whortleberries, or bilberries, which have unique medicinal qualities, grow everywhere. The juice of these berries is a regular part of the diet of our cosmonauts.

In addition to the usual representatives of Siberian wildlife, there are a number of unique animals that inhabit the steppe ravines and the mountains. There are the *dzeren* antelopes from the Mongolian deserts, a rare species of bobcat, and the red wolf. Tuva abounds in fur-bearing animals. The pelts of local sables, squirrels, ermines, and foxes often rank first at international auctions.

Under a heading called "Tradition and Beauty," the article continued:

The Bai-Taiga Mountains are famous for their ancient stonecutting traditions. They met me dressed up in clouds that the setting Sun had painted blue and purple—and left me one of those enchanted with the beauty of western Tuva for the rest of his life.

I found Saaya Koghel, a shepherd and a well-known sculptor, and his friend Donduk Doibukhaa, whose ancestors were sculptors too, in pastures high in the mountains. Koghel told me that finding the rare mineral *agal'matolit*[4] is about as difficult as carving a figure out of it. Deposits can be found locally only on the summit of one mountain, and they lie several meters deep.

"Here in Tuva a sculptor has to be a geologist and a mountain climber," Koghel remarked. "It's a challenge to find the stone, and then you've got to dig it up carefully and carry it down unharmed. *Chonardash*, which literally means carvable

---

[4]In English it is *pyrophillite*, identical in structure to soapstone but with aluminum replacing magnesium.

stone, has its secrets. It is perfectly pliable after it's dug up, but the stone becomes as hard as iron fairly soon. It may become black shot with silver, red, gold, or gray."

Miniature sculptures that repeat the themes of local lore have always been popular in Tuva.

There were no photographs of these stone carvings, but having seen Vainshtein's book on Tuvan art, we knew exactly what they looked like.

The article ended by raising a question:

> Why did the Tuvinians join the Soviet Union? To quote Salchak Toka, "The ethnically related nationalities who entered the Soviet Union at its very start are politically, economically, and culturally far ahead of us Tuvinians, their blood relatives, though they were at about the same level as we were before the Revolution."

On page seven of *Soviet Life* was an interview with Sevyan Vainshtein about a book he was writing called *The Mystery of Lake Tere-Khol.* Said Vainshtein:

> "The title is connected with the study of the mysterious ruins of an ancient fortress that has been preserved in Tuva on an island in Lake Tere-Khol, not far from the Soviet border with Mongolia. Although this unknown stone city in the upper reaches of the Yenisei River was already on the map of Siberia way back during the reign of Peter the great, it was not studied until the early fifties. The excavations, which I directed for several years, revealed a palace with tall columns, broad main staircases, and frescoes. The palace was built by Khan Moyun-Chur, a powerful ruler of the Uighur Khanate during the middle of the eighth century. It remains a riddle, however, how a formidable fortress with walls more than ten meters high that covers almost an entire island in the middle of a lake was built and how tons of building materials were

transported there by water. According to legend, the lake appeared after the fortress was built."

What a place! I looked for Tere-Khol on our Defense Mapping Agency navigation chart, and to my amazement found not one but two substantial lakes, about 125 miles apart, both with the name Tere-Khol. Was this a mistake? A Russian map I had Xeroxed at UCLA revealed the same information. Putting aside the problem of how the local people living between the two lakes answered the question "Which way is Tere-Khol?" I noticed that the lake to the east had an island in it, so I added it to the list of sights to see in Tuva.[5]

Suddenly the Chief said, "Hey, Ralph, look at this: 'American Botanists in Tuva'!"

"No way!" I protested, refusing to be taken in by a typical Feynman prank.

But there it was in bold print: **AMERICAN BOTA-NISTS IN TUVA.** The caption said:

> Participants in the Soviet-American botanic expedition in the Sayan Mountains. From left to right: Stanwyn G. Shetler, Valeri Nekrasov, David Murray, Thomas S. Elias, and Yuri Karapachinsky at the monument marking the center of the Asian continent.

The picture told the story: three Americans had reached the holiest of shrines in Kyzyl, and their names were not Richard Feynman, Ralph Leighton, and Glen Cowan.

---

[5]Since then I have found a Soviet map that indicates the lake to the west as "Tore Khol." According to the laws of Turkic "vowel harmony," this lake is probably "Töre Khöl" in Tuvan.

Meeting in Moscow

7 IT took me some time to regain my composure. Drumming helped some, but more helpful still was Richard reminding me of our goal. "We weren't trying to be first; we were just trying to get to Tuva—and we still are. At least we know now that it can be done."

"So, what should we do now—become botanists?" I asked.

"Not necessarily. But I think our chances would be better if we invented a legitimate reason to go—some purpose other than the fact that the capital of Tuva is spelled K-Y-Z-Y-L."

"Yeah," I said. "I know, I'll contact those botanists and find out how they got to Tuva."

At UCLA I looked through a faculty directory for U.S. colleges and universities and found Thomas Elias was at a college in Poughkeepsie, New York, while David Murray was at the University of Alaska in Fairbanks. There was no sign of Stanwyn Shelter. I wrote to Elias and

Murray; Murray wrote back that Elias was now the director of the Rancho Santa Ana botanical gardens at the Claremont Colleges in Pomona—less than an hour's drive from Pasadena!

I called up Dr. Elias and went out to meet him. He spoke in a soft monotone. "We go to the Soviet Union every other year under a bilateral agreement on environmental protection negotiated during the Nixon administration. We never know where we will be going until we get there—there's no point in asking for a particular place. We always go to some out-of-the-way place that tourists never see—that's where the good plants are. Last summer it happened to be Tuva."

"You mean you got to Tuva by chance?"

"I guess you could say that. The trip was arranged for us in Novosibirsk." Dr. Elias emphasized the idea of reciprocity. "The Soviets have no money to spend outside of the USSR, but they are eager to travel. So every other year we take them somewhere in the U.S. and pay for their stay here. They always pay for our expenses in the USSR."

I asked about the logistics of traveling in Tuva.

"There are typically several large trucks laden with supplies, and a staff of about a dozen workers who set up camp and prepare dinner for everyone. Soviet tents and sleeping bags are made of heavy canvas. You should bring your own sleeping bags."

I asked Dr. Elias if his group had heard any "throat" singing in Tuva.

"No."

Had they been inside a yurt?

"No."

Did they see any stellae with ancient Turkic runes?

"No."

Was the plant life interesting?

Dr. Elias's face lit up. "Oh, yes! I haven't had time to catalog all the samples we brought back."

I was dying to see some real Tuvan plants (especially the whortleberries that cosmonauts eat), but Dr. Elias said he had an appointment in a few minutes. As we parted he said, "Good luck."

In February 1985 we received a reply from Mr. Boslough. He reported that the *National Geographic* had already decided to do an article on Mongolia; Tuva was too similar. However, the writer on Mongolia would try to cross over the border and report on Tuva himself.

So much for our carefully honed letters and our best chance yet at reaching our beloved Tuva. I telephoned Glen and told him the news.

Undeterred, he had a suggestion. "Let's go to the Soviet Union anyway. This year is the fortieth anniversary of the end of World War II. If we go at the end of April, we can be there for the May Day parade and the VE parade eight days later."

I knew Richard wouldn't be interested. Besides, he was teaching a course which he was excited about, on computer theory. But I thought, Here's a chance to see some of the "Evil Empire," a chance to experience firsthand the system we're up against in trying to get to Tuva. I don't have to go as part of a tour group; instead I'll have my own personal guide who speaks Russian fluently. This is an opportunity not to be missed. I said, "You're on!"

The travel agent told us that Moscow and Leningrad were booked solid for the first two weeks of May—only VIPs could watch the parades in those cities.

I wanted to propose Abakan, but I knew it was out of the question: once there, I would be tempted to make a dash for Tuva that could get us thrown in jail.

"What about Volgograd?" suggested Glen. "The Battle of Stalingrad [as the city was called during Stalin's rule] was the turning point for the Soviets in World War II. Besides, it would be interesting to see what an average city in the heart of

Russia is like." I had learned by then that even average places are interesting, so I agreed.

"There's space available in Volgograd," said the agent. "Where else would you like to go?"

"How about the Caucasus?" I said. I had become interested in that part of the world from the Armenian students in my classes. Glen approved, and suggested we relax a few days on the "Red Riviera" (the Black Sea coast) on our way back to Moscow.

Despite the long distances involved, we wanted to travel only by train. We were both nervous about air travel in the USSR, since the authorities never reported accidents. "Besides, Soviet trains are cool," said Glen. "They're a great place to meet people and talk."

The travel agent talked us into adding "transfers"—an extra $50 each—because taxis were often hard to find. But the airfare to Helsinki, where we would board the train that would take us into the USSR, was quite expensive. When I got back to Pasadena I went to the Caltech library and found some bargain fares from Heathrow to Helsinki in the London *Times* and purchased our tickets by phone with a credit card. We then booked a flight to London on World Airways.

In early March Konstantin Chernenko died, by now expectedly. As yet another state funeral was being planned for Red Square, jokes surfaced in Moscow about a loyal Soviet citizen asking, "Can I purchase a season pass?"

In the preceding weeks there had been talk of a power struggle: would the top post of General Secretary go to old conservative Victor Grishin (the one who wrote me the year before), to young conservative Grigoriy Romanov (who Kremlinologists thought was in the strongest position), or to Andropov's pragmatic protégé Mikhail Gorbachev? At Chernenko's funeral the lineup of the Politburo on top of Lenin's tomb revealed the winner: Mikhail S. Gorbachev. (Romanov remained on the Politburo for another four months. Grishin held on until January 1986, when he was replaced by Boris Yeltsin.)

To help me prepare for the USSR, Richard lent me a book off his shelf called *The Russians,* by Hedrick Smith. "I think you'll find it interesting," he said. Given the Chief's disdain for politics, I was surprised that he even possessed such a book.

Among many interesting things, the book mentioned a cemetery in Moscow (closed to everyone but special tourist groups and relatives of those buried there) full of Russian scientists and writers. Khrushchev was buried there, too— unlike Lenin, Stalin, and Brezhnev, whose remains were interred on Red Square. As I carefully printed NOVODEVICHI at the top of my list for sights to see in Moscow, I remembered a poem by Marianne Moore I had cut out from *Life* magazine when I was in high school:

I May, I Might, I Must

If you will tell me why the fen
appears impassable, I then
will tell you why I think that I
can get across it if I try.

At the end of April Glen and I left Oakland and Los Angeles, respectively. The next day we arrived in a snow flurry in Helsinki. Glen was excited—it was the first snowfall he had ever seen. Later the sky turned blue, so we walked around Helsinki in the light of the slowly setting northern sun. It seemed as if we were already in Russia: a statue of Czar Alexander II, whose empire had stretched from Finland to Alaska, dominated a cobblestone square surrounded by finely designed ocher-colored buildings; on a nearby hill stood a Russian Orthodox church complete with an onion-shaped dome and glistening gold crosses that looked like bent TV aerials.

The next morning we purchased our tickets to Leningrad and proceeded to the wide-gauge tracks leading to the USSR. Glen remarked that these were probably the very tracks on which Lenin slipped into czarist Russia (in a boxcar) from exile in Switzerland. After a few hours we stopped just before the border. The Finnish locomotive pulled away from the train. As the red star of the Soviet locomotive came into view, I couldn't resist taking a picture. "Ralph!" Glen whispered in horror. "Pictures of Soviet trains are forbidden!"

"But we're still in Finland," I protested.

"You're bringing your film *into* the Soviet Union," Glen countered.

I took the picture anyway, but then put my camera away— it was the only way I could resist taking the rows of border fences that other passengers furtively photographed.

Two Soviet border guards entered our train compartment and went through our luggage. Of most interest to them were two copies of *Surely You're Joking, Mr. Feynman!*, which had just been published. One was for Sevyan Vainshtein; the other was for a Soviet publisher in the hope that a Russian translation of the infamous Feynman stories would appear. Glen explained something to the guards about "Feynman, fizika," and "Nobel."

The older guard found the list of sights I wanted to see. The only word printed clearly was the forbidden cemetery in Moscow whose name I could barely pronounce: NOVODEVICHI.

He pointed to it and looked at me, his eyes asking, "Why Novodevichi?"

Before Glen could explain anything, I said, "Khrushchev."

The guard's face flushed crimson, but his eyes showed understanding, even sympathy. He handed the paper back to me and motioned to the younger guard that the inspection was over.

We packed our bags and relaxed. Glen set his watch forward sixty minutes as the scenery outside set out thoughts back sixty years: nestled in the birch forest were brightly colored dachas, mostly blue, adorned with intricate shingle work and white window frames; each house had a well with a crankshaft, rope, and bucket.

The chambermaid of our train car brought us glasses of tasty Georgian tea. After we finished, I took the glasses back to her. She promptly swished them around in a "germ bath" (as Glen called it), a tub of lukewarm water. Before they had a chance to dry, she filled our glasses with tea for the next group of passengers. I was not surprised when I came down with a sore throat a few days later.

We were met at the Leningrad train station by our "transfer"—an Intourist taxi—and taken outside of town to a large motel whose main purpose evidently was to provide busloads of Finns with old-fashioned dancing and cheap vodka. After dinner we took a city bus into Leningrad. As night fell, the city of three and a half million forgot to turn on the lights: Leningrad seemed to be under a wartime blackout—virtually no traffic, everything subdued. Glen and I lowered our voices to a whisper to fit in with the strolling shadows. Only the occasional clang of a tram punctuated the somber silence.

The next morning brought a sunny day. We walked briskly along the famous canals, and thought of Dr. Anna Maenchen as we passed through the historic archway where the "Great October Revolution" had begun, into the square where the pastel blue Hermitage ran for an entire block. (We decided not to go inside; there was simply too much to see.) Outside were draped huge red banners, thirty feet high, with hammer-and-sickle emblems and portraits of Marx, Engels, and Lenin. May Day was approaching.

Down at the Neva River, sports enthusiasts played volleyball in their swim trunks. Although the sun was shining, the temperature was only barely in the thirties. A man we called Jack Lalanski[1] performed ritual push-ups on the sandy beach before calmly entering the chilly water to swim among the large, crackling chunks of ice.

After returning to our motel in the evening for dinner, we were driven to the train station in our "transfer" and dropped off in front. We milled around for a couple of hours inside. As we boarded our midnight train to Moscow, a man suddenly appeared and said, "Mr. Cowan, Mr. Leighton?"

"Da, da," said Glen.

"Here is your train. Follow me to your compartment." The man introduced us to the train car conductor, and disappeared into the night.

Glen offered an explanation for this unnerving experience: the man was supposed to have met us at the front of the station when our "transfer" dropped us off. But our driver was so eager to get away that the connection was missed.

We rolled into Moscow at 8 A.M. This time our "transfer" was a black Chaika automobile like the ones assigned to government officials. Private automobiles were any color except black, making it easy to tell who was entitled to use the special express lanes in the middle of large thoroughfares. We were whisked from the Leningrad station to the Hotel Metropol, smack in the center of town. We would have five hours to wander around. (With May Day only forty-eight hours away, NVIPs like us could not stay in Moscow overnight.)

We walked past the infamous sign—now less menacing than laughable—that proclaimed "Communism Will Triumph Over the Whole World!" and entered Red Square. To our left the GUM—the Gosudarstvennyi Universal'nyi Magazin (Moscow's original shopping mall)—was bedecked with huge red canvasses full of slogans and emblems, which were themselves dwarfed by a hundred-foot-tall banner of

[1]Jack Lalanne was the original Southern California Muscle Beach body-building buff.

Lenin. To our right was Lenin's tomb, with the Kremlin wall looming behind. At the far end of the square stood the distinctive domes of St. Basil's Cathedral.

As TV technicians on platforms tested their equipment, we realized we had walked onto a big movie set. We imagined Mr. Gorbachev and the rest of the Politburo, lined up on Lenin's tomb, reviewing the workers' brigades marching across the cobblestones below, where we stood.

A tour group disembarking from a bus caught my eye: most of the men were wearing distinctive hats decorated with motifs straight out of Vainshtein's book on Tuvan art. "Glen!" I exclaimed, pointing excitedly. "Tuvans!"

I rushed over and reached the group just before it entered St. Basil's Cathedral. I made eye contact with one of the men and said, "Ekii!"

The man was startled but said nothing.

I was sure I had pronounced the Tuvan greeting correctly—after all, Ondar had been able to understand it over a crackly phone line from Oakland to Kyzyl. But just in case I had it wrong, I said, "Tyva—Kyzyl?"

The man smiled. My heart pounded. "Kirghiz!" he said, proudly.[2]

The man began speaking to me in Russian. I looked for Glen to translate, but he was nowhere to be seen.

At the appointed hour we returned to the Hotel Metropol, got into our waiting limousine, and sped past KGB headquarters and its infamous Lubyanka Prison to Kazan station. The baton passed smoothly: we were met by an Intourist guide who led us to our train compartment.

We arrived twenty-six hours later in Volgograd. Despite the warm and pleasant weather, the trees at the railroad sta-

[2]The Kirghiz are a Turkic people whose ancestors inhabited Tuva for several centuries. Today they live a thousand miles to the southwest, in and near the Pamir Mountains, though their name remains in Tuva as a clan name: Kyrgys.

tion scarcely showed a sign of spring. The Intourist greeter immediately spoke to Glen in Russian.

"How did you know I speak Russian?" he asked.

"Moscow telegraphed me that the taller one speaks Russian; the other one does not."

Our "transfer" was ridiculous: the hotel was across the square from the railroad station, less than a hundred yards away. Nevertheless, we rode in a small Intourist bus reserved just for us.

When we entered our fourth-floor room, we heard voices just outside our window. I leaned out and saw several workers attaching huge red banners to the adjoining balconies. Below, loudspeakers barked instructions at groups of boisterous parade participants who pushed and tugged a meandering caravan of large decorated carts across the huge square, in front of a row of Politburo portraits, central among which was that of Mr. Gorbachev—minus the prominent birthmark on his forehead.

As we strolled around Volgograd that evening, I realized that Russia's heartland lay on the western end of the vast Eurasian steppe. With the Kalmyk Mongol Autonomous Republic only thirty miles away and Kazakhstan less than one hundred, the faces of many Russians revealed Mongolian and Turkic features. The only thing that could make me forget the exotic beauty of a woman from Volgograd was the sight of another beautiful woman from Volgograd.

May Day was overcast and windy with light, intermittent showers. I figured our balcony offered the best vantage point for the parade, but a chambermaid sent us downstairs. We went outside and watched thousands of people, from Young Pioneers to workers' brigades, assemble along three avenues leading into the square. The participants vastly outnumbered the spectators—mainly Party dignitaries—who lined the hundred-yard-long route.

As the May Day parade began, Glen and I found a place to

stand, behind a line of policemen. Each group was introduced by a voice on the loudspeakers. Then came a slogan, such as "Forward into the future with communism!"

The brigade would respond "oo-RAAAH!" The routine repeated itself a hundred times.

A young Soviet and his girlfriend approached us and said a few words in English. Glen switched into Russian, while I started up a conversation with a young woman next to them who was obviously not a Soviet. A foreign exchange student from Madagascar who could speak English and French in addition to Russian and Malagasy, she was in her third year of Russian language study in Volgograd, and would not be able to return home, even for vacation, for another two years.

As the rain fell harder, we all headed into a coffeehouse. We were joined by some Soviet medical students who promptly lit up their pungent, Soviet cigarettes. Eventually the rain stopped—about the same time the parade was over—so we walked down to the Volga River to watch the merriment, mostly in the form of public drinking and dancing.

The next morning, at breakfast, Glen and I noticed several long tables in the hotel restaurant decorated with Soviet and American flags. Two delegations entered and took their places: the Soviet delegation consisted of a dozen elderly Soviet veterans in uniforms covered with medals; most of the Americans were younger and less formally attired—some wore denim jackets with ban-the-bomb symbols. After breakfast an Intourist guide announced that buses were waiting outside. We asked if we could tag along, and she agreed.

It turned out to be a special tour for a group of American veterans who had already met their Soviet counterparts for a ceremony at the Elbe River, where American and Soviet forces had linked up forty years before. One of the Americans showed me an article from *Time* about it.

The Soviets had hoped President Reagan would meet Mikhail Gorbachev for the occasion. Instead, Reagan went to England and France to commemorate the Invasion of Normandy, and then to a cemetery in Bitburg, Germany, where several young men of Hitler's SS were buried. In his speeches, Reagan scarcely mentioned the Soviet war effort.

After the sobering experience of touring Soviet war memorials, we proceeded to a nearby park where we watched the two delegations plant a tree of friendship from Kansas, the home state of General Eisenhower.

The next day we were to begin our journey to Baku. The logical route was via Rostov, 200 miles to the west. But since the direct line to Rostov was not an "Intourist route," we had to retrace 600 miles to Moscow, change trains, and then travel another 600 miles to reach Rostov—an additional 1000 miles in all.

We explained to the Intourist guide that our train to Volgograd had been six hours late. Given that we had only five hours to make our connection in Moscow, what if our train was late again?

"Do not worry," she said. "Trains are only late going *out* of Moscow. They are never late coming *in* to Moscow." Later I learned that the Russians have an expression for such obvious lying: "coming out of the water dry."

Intourist regulations required that we go to the train station an hour before departure. Because the station was literally a stone's throw from the hotel, we said we would gladly walk the hundred yards on our own, so our Intourist bus driver could take a holiday.

Nyet. The hotel porter put our bags in the little bus, whereupon we rode for one minute to the station and stood on the platform with our friendly Intourist guide—who wasn't about to leave us until we were safely aboard our train.

The twenty-hour ride to Moscow was pleasant enough, except for the aroma of dried, salted fish that our Russian compartment companions generously shared with us. Glen perfected his Russian, while I perfected surreptitious picture-taking. The train arrived on time in Moscow.

Intourist transferred us from the Kazan station to the Kiev station, and showed us to our train. As we walked along the platform, we were treated to a course in Soviet socioeconomics: the train cars destined for Kharkov and Rostov (in the Ukraine and Russia) were new and clean; the cars destined for Baku (capital of Moslem Azerbaijan) were old and dirty. I joked, "Here's our car, Glen. I can read the sign all by myself: it says 'S-E-L-M-A.' "

Our compartment compatriots were a Vietnamese student studying oil technology in Baku, and an Azeri soldier—from whom Glen learned plenty of Russian expressions not found in textbooks. The only surprise on our thirty-six-hour ride was the sudden appearance of a mustachioed deaf-mute who handed out black-and-white photographs for passengers to buy: of the half-dozen choices (including a buxom Indian goddess), the most popular was Joseph Stalin.

We rolled past Sumgaït, last outpost of Europe, into Baku—gateway to Asia and former oil capital of the world.[3] The weather was hot and smoggy; unlike Moscow and Leningrad, the streets were choked with traffic. I felt right at home.

When we checked into our ninth-floor room at the modern, sixteen-story hotel, we found our view blocked by a huge canvas portrait of Lenin that covered an area six rooms wide and eight floors high. I preferred a view of the smog, so we got our room changed. On the huge square below, a marching band prepared for the upcoming VE Day festivities.

In the late afternoon, as the air cooled slowly, we walked around the old quarter past children playing soccer in the winding alleys. I heard some words of Armenian, which re-

---

[3]Sadly, these cities would become famous in 1988 and 1990 for the massacres of Armenians by Azeris and of Azeris by Soviet troops.

minded me that Baku was the home of the young, flamboyant chess champion Garo Kasparian—né Weinstein (his father's name), better known to the world as Gary Kasparov (the Russian version of his mother's name).

On the afternoon of May 8 (which was not VE Day, as victory over Germany was announced in the USSR on May 9), we were transferred to the train station for an overnight trip to Tbilisi. I knew we had crossed into neighboring Georgia when we saw a familiar portrait for the first time on a public building: that of Joseph Stalin ("Joe Steel"), a.k.a. Jozef Dzhugashvili, Georgia's (in)famous native son.

In Tbilisi our Intourist taxi passed through one road block after another to reach our hotel, situated once again on the city's main square. The VE Day parade was already in progress. In addition to Young Pioneers, army recruits, and workers' brigades, there were folk groups of swashbuckling men and graceful women in dazzling costumes, performing dances of the Caucasus and singing Georgian songs. Foremost among the distinguished spectators lined up on a balcony overlooking the square was Georgian Communist Party Chief Eduard Shevardnadze.

The next day I went over to the post office and sent a telegram to Richard—his birthday was coming up on May 11. As Glen convalesced in the hotel with some sort of flu, I wandered around the old part of town. Whereas the air in Baku was hot, humid, and smoggy, the air in Tbilisi, though hot, was dry and clear—industry was kept outside of town. A score of twelve-sided Armenian and Georgian churches stood proudly against the brilliant blue sky.

In the late afternoon I happened to pass a synagogue. I peered in just in time to see several hundred men of all ages, dressed in black, hurriedly chant a prayer (it was a Friday) and bolt for the door as if competing in a foot race.

Outside, as the setting sun threw its last light over the city, a young, tall, bearded man—a Lutheran seminary student from Estonia—approached and said he wanted to practice speaking English. "We Estonians prefer English to Russian," he said. The young man had been traveling all over the Soviet Union by train for the past two months. "As long as you don't stay overnight in a hotel, you don't have to show any documents," he explained. Thus he slept only on trains, or in the homes of local citizens in the places he wanted to stay for more than a day.

On Sunday Glen and I took a funicular to Stalin Park, high above Old Tbilisi. In addition to beautiful gardens and shady paths for lovers of all ages, there was an amusement park, a restaurant with a spectacular view, and plenty of shish-kebab stands. I spotted an ice cream parlor. As my mouth watered, Glen politely asked in beautiful Russian what flavors were available. In typical Soviet fashion the woman ignored him and began speaking to a co-worker. Then she decided to do some washing up. I put on a smile and spoke to her in English, gesturing in broad strokes: "Hello, we'd like some ice cream." I pointed at Glen and said, "American." Immediately she served us with a smile.

In the evening we boarded the overnight train to Yerevan, Armenia. The sun rose as we clanked along the Arpa River, once an insignificant tributary of the Araxes River in the middle of eastern Armenia, but now the border with Turkey and NATO.

For once our hotel was not on the main square. Instead, it stood in a veritable slum at the edge of town. After visiting the poignant memorial to the Armenian holocaust of 1915, we returned to our hotel to watch the sunset. As mothers prepared dinner in roofless kitchens and children played in the dusty street below, the two peaks of spectacular 17,000-foot Mount Ararat, just over the border in Turkey, emerged from the haze of another hot day in that godforsaken land.

The next morning we accompanied a tour group to nearby Echmiadzin, the religious center of Armenia. The sight of bearded monks in full regalia reminded me that Armenia was first to adopt Christianity as its official religion. (Legend has it that Georgia and Ethiopia were next.) While the group visited a church, Glen and I went to a nearby cemetery. Most of the gravestones had photographs etched into them. Right away we noticed several young men pictured in military uniform who died in the early 1980s, presumably in Afghanistan.

That afternoon we located, after considerable effort, some paintings by Eduard Kazarian, an eccentric violist in the Yerevan Symphony. Some of his work had been displayed in a big exposition touring the United States that trumpeted Soviet achievements in science and technology. But what the crowds lined up for hours to see—through powerful magnifying glasses—was Kazarian's intricate work, including a statue of Charlie Chaplin (standing inside the eye of a needle), and a caravan of circus—animals painted on a single human hair. Kazarian's brush was a single mohair; the strokes were applied between heartbeats. He was broadening a tradition, born in the days when Christians were persecuted, of rendering religious works in miniature.

The Kazarian miniatures we found in Yerevan included a series of scenes painted on the spikes of an ear of wheat. The glass cases that "protected" these remarkable works of art collected dust on the ledge of a tall bookcase, ready to fall to the floor in the next earthquake.

That night we visited the family of a physicist Glen had met at Berkeley. They sent over a "taxi" to pick us up. As the private car pulled up to our hotel, we realized there were very few official taxis in Yerevan. I postulated that any private car was a potential taxi. (We gathered a data point two days later: I put out my hand; within seconds a car screeched to a halt and picked us up.) When I tried to pay the driver, he recoiled as if my money was radioactive. From various gestures I discovered that the customer should carelessly drop one or two rubles on the floor.

The family stopped at nothing to please their guests: six courses of food, most of it produce gathered from the family dacha, were each introduced by a toast followed by a shot of Armenian cognac. Local custom called for the men at the table to stand up for each round. After the toast, it was strictly bottoms up. Glen diplomatically got out of it, pleading a genetic predisposition to alcoholism. When it was my turn, I made a short toast in Russian and Armenian: "Granitsa—hisoon kilometer!" (Border—fifty kilometers!) We all raised our glasses to the return of Mount Ararat to Armenia.

The next day a friend of our hosts drove us to a monastery built into the cliffs of a remote valley. Dozens of white handkerchiefs and strips of cloth were tied to nearby bushes as an offering to the mountain spirits, a pagan practice that survived both Christianity and Marxism.

The next morning we boarded the train and retraced our route to Tbilisi. We passed through cities and towns whose names would spell disaster in a powerful earthquake three and a half years later: Leninakan, Spitak, Kirovakan.

We arrived in Sochi, a resort on the "Red Riviera," at 6 A.M. For once we were not greeted by a "transfer." We happily hailed a regular taxi and drove into town.

We saw buildings going up all over Sochi. They looked like great houses of cards, with prefabricated concrete slabs placed one on top of another—up to seventeen stories. To add to my nervousness Glen pointed out the cement trucks—their drums did not rotate.

When we appeared at our hotel, the clerk was horrified. "We thought your train was coming at 6 P.M.," she said. Just to see what would happen, we asked for reimbursement of our taxi fare. Impossible: our "transfers" were paid with some sort of coupon which could not be converted into money (at least for us).

The Black Sea coast is a popular vacation spot for Soviets, who go not with their families but with their fellow workers (to the regret of some, to the relief of others)—a fact made fleshly to us by the solicitous looks we got from pairs of Soviet women in the hotel dining room.

As we explored Sochi's environs, we realized that the Red Riviera is one big summer camp. There are arrows on well-marked paths, with numbers representing the degree of difficulty. Large signs from the Department of Recreation and Leisure explain how to take a walk: "Swing your arms thus and so [pictures showed exactly how], stand erect, breathe deeply, . . ."

We came upon an uncrowded restaurant—no tour buses happened to be there at the moment—so we decided to have lunch. After three weeks in the USSR, we had the restaurant routine down pat:

1. Don't be surprised if three or four waiters—healthy, strong young men fit for construction work—look right through you for ten minutes. They are hard at work deciding which one of them will come over and tell you, "This table is not in service."
2. After you move to another table, don't get indignant if the waiters then decide their most urgent task is to wipe the already-dry wine glasses on the long table set up for thirty people.
3. When it becomes obvious that you will not leave—this will happen fastest if you look like you are enjoying yourself—you will finally get some attention.
4. Don't let your mouth start watering by taking the menu seriously. Despite the respectable list of entrees, only one will be available. Simply ask, "What does the chef recommend today?"
5. Expect potatoes with every meal. For raw vegetables, you'd better like radishes and cucumbers.
6. If you are still hungry after the meager portions you've been served, order extra bread.
7. Expect to pay for each pat of butter. But don't worry, it's cheap—you are enjoying a small part of the huge butter mountain subsidized by the European Economic Community.
8. Expect the paper "napkins"—single-layer triangles torn diago-

nally from a double-layer square original—to last for only one wipe of the mouth. You will end up using at least four, the equivalent of one original napkin.

9. Be sure to carry every possible combination of coins and bills; somehow the cash register always runs out of change just before you pay.

The next day we boarded the train once again, this time for the thirty-hour trip to Moscow. We looked forward to the good eating on the train: the soup, cooked for hours—perhaps days—and served steaming hot with bread, is a real treat.

When we checked into our hotel in Moscow, there were postcards waiting for us from Sevyan Vainshtein and Lev Okun, a prominent physicist whose book, *Leptons and Quarks,* Glen had used in his graduate studies. Each gave us his telephone number. We were able to contact Okun right away so we set up a meeting with him for the following morning.

Okun was interested in publishing a Russian version of Feynman's latest book, *QED: The Strange Theory of Light and Matter.* He also wanted to publish a Russian version of *Surely You're Joking, Mr. Feynman!* "Our people need to become acquainted with Feynman's mentality," he said.

Publishing Feynman's irreverent humor in the Soviet Union was a bit tricky, however. All the publishers that Okun had contacted had turned him down. But he had a suggestion: "If you wouldn't mind going over to Mir publishers yourselves, I'm sure they would be happy to meet you."

It was true. We got an appointment for three o'clock that afternoon. Okun politely declined to go with us; perhaps the importance of this meeting with foreigners—in the eyes of the Mir editors—would be diminished by the presence of an eminent Soviet physicist.

We made our way by subway and taxi to the editorial offices of Mir publishers, located in a neighborhood of former stately residences. We were met by two senior editors, who presented us with lapel pins. A secretary prepared tea. We learned that Mir's Russian translation of *The Feynman Lectures on Physics* had been their biggest success—more than one million copies published over the past twenty years.

I mentioned that Professor Feynman might come to the USSR in a year or two. (I refrained from mentioning Tuva, in case the Mir editors did not share our enthusiasm for the place.) The editors said Mir could make some rubles available to Feynman—a kind of delayed royalty payment—even though they were not obliged to do so. (The Russian translation had come out before the USSR joined the International Copyright Convention.)

We pulled out a copy of *Surely You're Joking*. The editors were very interested to read it, but not sure about publishing it. "We publish only technical books," they said.

After our meeting with Mir, we went to the Novodevichi monastery, which was open to the public, and then to the gates of the Novodevichi cemetery in the hope of seeing Khrushchev's grave. I tried entering with a group being waved in, but was stopped by a guard.

Thwarted, I decided to attempt a more modest goal. Since our first day in the Soviet Union I had watched with horror as one person after another drank from the communal cup of a coin-operated mineral water machine. Now, having drunk innumerable dirty glasses of tea on trains, I was prepared for my initiation. Like a native I stood behind a man I had never seen before, and waited patiently for him to finish drinking. He turned the glass upside down and pressed it onto a small rack, causing some tap water to spit up into it. When he walked away, I stepped up to the machine and threw a 3-kopek coin into the slot. Without hesitation I tanked the mildly fizzy water (a bit salty), and pressed the glass down on the rack. Mission accomplished.

As I walked away, I thought, Maybe communal glasses keep everyone's immune system revved up. After an initial invest-ment of a few sore throats, you're able to fight off the colds and flus of winter. (Over the next week nothing happened—not even another sore throat.)

The next day, Glen and I finally made contact with Sevyan Vainshtein by telephone from a pay booth just off Red Square. He suggested meeting at the Akademia subway stop.

We met Vainshtein at the appointed hour. He had a warm smile and a twinkle in his eye that reminded us of Feynman. We learned later there were other similarities: both men came from Jewish families but were not believers; both had non-Jewish wives. Vainshtein's family was long established in Riga; Feynman's grandparents had come from Minsk.

Vainshtein led us around the corner and down the block to the Institute of Ethnography, housed in what appeared to be an old private secondary school: the four-story wooden building was poorly lit; the hallway floors creaked. Most of the ethnographers at the institute were Russian, but several Asians—Kazakh, Kirghiz, and others—were also in evidence. After introducing us around as his "colleagues" from the United States (but never showing us into the director's of-fice), Vainshtein invited us to sit in on a thesis defense by a doctoral candidate whose topic was the Ket people of Siberia.

Vainshtein handed Glen his copy of the thesis. It was barely legible, because it had been bashed out on a mechani-cal typewriter—under at least two layers of overused carbon paper. After a rather harsh grilling by the others about the questionable significance of studying a tribe of only three hundred people, the hapless candidate got sympathetic treat-ment from Vainshtein, who pointed out that small groups of people can hold the key to historical mysteries. (The candi-date did not pass, nonetheless.) That done, Vainshtein in-vited us to his apartment the following night.

The next day at about five o'clock, we met Vainshtein

again at the Institute of Ethnography—he figured it would be difficult for us to find his apartment on our own. As we entered the Akademia subway station with him, he asked us how much the metro costs in California. Familiar with the Bay Area Rapid Transit system, Glen said, "One or two dollars, depending on how far you go."

Vainshtein pulled out a handful of change from his pocket and threw three 5-kopek coins into a turnstile as each of us went through. "Still the same price as when it was built," he said, proudly.

I tried to explain that a price that low obviously meant that the people in the provinces were heavily subsidizing the Moscow subway—but my high school German didn't serve me well, and Glen wouldn't translate my comment into Russian.

As we rode the noisy trains for the better part of an hour, I could hardly hear myself think. Meanwhile, Glen was having a great conversation with Vainshtein, even understanding his jokes.

After we ascended from the last subway station, we took a bus for fifteen minutes or so. It dropped us off in a district of nondescript five-story apartment houses. We arrived around 7 P.M. at Vainshtein's third-floor apartment.

Vainshtein introduced us to his wife and to his mother, who also lived in his apartment. His daughter (their only child) was not at home; she lived at a university away from Moscow.

We went into the study. Vainshtein showed us various Tuvanalia, including his collection of stone carvings. On the wall was a beautiful oil painting, full of reds and purples, of a sunset in the Sayan Mountains. Vainshtein had painted it himself. "Tuwa ist sehr schön," he said, pronouncing "schön" the way Wayne Newton did when he sang, "Dan-ku shane, I said dan-ku shane . . ."

Vainshtein didn't need to convince us that Tuva is beautiful. I wanted to ask him what became of the news that he and the director of his institute were arranging Feynman's trip to Tuva. But I figured the idea must have fallen through—else he would have said something by now—and there was no point in beating a dead horse.

Vainshtein pulled a museum catalog down from his bookcase. It was written in Japanese and English. He said in German, "I sent a copy to Professor Feynman. Did he receive it?"

I said no, scratching my head.

Then he pulled down another museum catalog, this one in Finnish and English, and said, "I sent a copy of *this* catalog to Professor Feynman also. Did he receive it?"

No again.

Vainshtein explained that the catalogs were from an exhibition organized by the USSR Academy of Sciences that had traveled to Japan in 1982 and to Finland earlier in 1985. Called "On the Silk Road," the exhibition contained several hundred archaeological objects, many unearthed by Vainshtein himself in Tuva.

It was time for dinner.

We entered the dining room and found three other guests. There were two young women: one was Russian, the other Asian—from Buryatia, the region near Lake Baikal inhabited by people related to the Mongols. The young woman from Buryatia had just completed her doctoral work under Vainshtein's guidance. The dinner was in her honor, and here Vainshtein had been talking to us all this time, ignoring her!

Fortunately, both young women were being well attended to by a charming and handsome Russian (one of Vainshtein's colleagues at the Institute of Ethnography), who was holding forth with entertaining stories à la Feynman—about his days as a sailor, about his experiences in Australia, the South Seas, England, and Japan. We took our seats at the table.

The table was full of bite-size food: three types of caviar, ornately carved cucumbers, sliced sausage, sliced tomatoes, some sort of quiche, rice pudding, custard, biscuits, and more—all complemented by several types of vodka and co-gnac.

The conversation—in German, Russian, and English—was punctuated frequently by a toast from each of the men. Vainshtein began by offering a toast to Feynman. After some more conversation, Glen rose to salute Vainshtein's wife for the delicious meal she had prepared.

Then Vainshtein told a story. While he was the director of a museum in Kyzyl, he met a young Russian woman who had been sent to Tuva as an elementary school teacher. She said her birthday was in three days, and perhaps he would like to come to her house for a small party she was having.

When the day came, Vainshtein went to the local bakery and looked for a birthday cake. The baker showed Vainshtein the only cake in the store, ordered by a man who was going to propose marriage that evening. "If the customer doesn't come for it by closing time, it's yours," the baker said.

At closing time Vainshtein came back. The cake was still there.

"Shall I change the letters to HAPPY BIRTHDAY?" the baker asked.

"Uh, sure," replied Vainshtein. "On second thought, leave it the way it is: proposing to her is not a bad idea!"

"And I've been stuck with him ever since!" chimed in Mrs. Vainshtein with a smile on her face, delivering the punch line to a story she had undoubtedly heard a hundred times.

After some more eating, it was my turn to deliver a toast. I felt uncomfortable that Glen and I were receiving so much attention on this occasion intended to congratulate Vainshtein's graduate student. It reminded me of a joke I had seen in MAD magazine, where a kid in "Berg's Eye View" says, "You're just like a blister: you show up just after the hard work is done!"

The problem was, I couldn't translate the joke into German. I appealed to Glen to translate it into Russian, but he whispered, "No, Ralph; it's stupid. They'll never get it."

I couldn't think of anything else to say in my toast, so I insisted. Glen finally asked Vainshtein's colleague, who knew English quite well, what the Russian word for blister was. He said he didn't know. Then I described a blister to Vainshtein in German, and he understood what it was, but claimed not to know the Russian word for it either. Was this some sort of taboo word for academics—as if knowing the word for blister meant you had once worked with your hands?

I did the best I could to describe the joke but—as Glen warned me—it was stupid, and the Soviets didn't get it.

After more trilingual talk, it was Vainshtein's colleague's turn to deliver a toast. His salute to the virtues of women had the men in stitches and the women flushing with embarrassment. As his toast went on, I began to wonder about him—he was so smooth and cavalier. I had read that any meeting a Soviet has with a foreigner must be reported to the KGB. Was Vainshtein saving himself some trouble by inviting the KGB man to dinner?

By the time the charmer's speech had ended, I was sober and ready for another drink. We raised our glasses and bottomed up.

After dinner I pulled out a copy of *Surely You're Joking*, presented it to Vainshtein, and described the visit Glen and I had paid to Mir publishers.

"Professor Feynman is well known in our country," replied Vainshtein, who recounted how he was traveling in western Tuva recently, and met a young Tuvan woman sitting outside a yurt. Her name was Marx Kyrgys. (I supposed her parents had heard the name "Marx" bandied about, so they named her after the great white hero—much like many freed slaves were named after presidents.) Marx was studying to be a teacher. And the book she was reading? *The Feynman Lectures on Physics!*

"The Chief is gonna love that story," I said to Glen, as we all raised a glass of after-dinner liqueur to Richard.

As conversation continued, I asked Vainshtein if it was true he was preparing a book about a Uighur fortress on an island in Lake Tere-Khol.

"Yes," he said. "How did you know?"

I pulled out a copy of *Soviet Life* that I had brought along and showed him the article.

"I don't remember speaking to anyone from this magazine," he said. "And I've never heard of that reporter. Yet the information is basically correct." He offered an explanation: the reporter must have seen an interview that Vainshtein had given to another publication, and simply wrote the article from that.

He gave me a Finnish copy of "On the Silk Road," and said, "This exhibition will be going to Göteborg, Sweden, in February of next year."

I looked at the *Soviet Life* magazine again and saw the article about the American botanists in Tuva. I remembered the Chief's advice—that we have to find a reason to go to Tuva (*other* than the fact that its capital is spelled K-Y-Z-Y-L)—and suddenly realized that Vainshtein had just handed us our reason. I raised an imaginary glass and proclaimed, "After Sweden, the exhibition will come to the United States—and as members of the host museum, Richard Feynman, Ralph Leighton, and Glen Cowan will visit Tuva with Sevyan Vainshtein!"

Amateur Ambassadors

8   GLEN flew back to Berkeley, while I took the train to Bochum, Germany, to visit my brother, Alan—he was first horn in the symphony orchestra there—and his wife, Linda. Then I went to Göteborg, Sweden, to visit a physicist who had stayed with our family nearly twenty years before as a student in the Experiment for International Living.

The early June weather was spectacular. Clear, sunny skies and temperatures in the eighties brought the whole population out to the rocky coastline, whose latitude is the same as the panhandle of Alaska. So many women sunbathed topless that it quickly became no big deal to the neophyte observer from prudish North America.

Perhaps because I was dazzled by the bright, warm days of a Swedish spring, it never occurred to me to go down to the Göteborg Historical Museum, where the Silk Road exhibition would make its appearance eight months later. Besides, I assumed that a traveling exhibition was like a traveling circus: it rolls into town in the middle of the week; by Friday everything is set up and the public comes to see the show. Had I understood anything about the museum business, I would have known that preparations for the Silk Road exhibition were already well under way.

When I got back to Pasadena I told the Chief about my plan to bring the Silk Road exhibition to the United States, and showed him a copy of the exhibition catalog Vainshtein had tried to send him. "And by the way," I said, "did you get the birthday telegram I sent you from Tbilisi?"

"No, I didn't get any telegrams."

"How about the two postcards?"

"I didn't get any postcards, either."

"That's strange," I said. "Everybody else I've checked with got the postcards I sent them; it's a miracle that Vainshtein's New Year's greetings got through to you at Caltech. I wonder how much other stuff never made it."

I didn't do anything about Tuva or the Silk Road exhibition during the entire summer 1985—or during the fall, when I took up teaching again. Perhaps I was still burned out from all the trains, "transfers," and surly Soviet waiters Glen and I had endured in the USSR. At any rate, I didn't even get the hint to dust off the exhibition catalog when, in November of 1985, Ronald Reagan met Mikhail Gorbachev for the first time and announced that the result of their meeting in Geneva was a cultural agreement under which an exhibition of forty French Impressionist paintings would come to the United States.

The new year began for the Friends of Tuva with no indication that anything would be different in 1986. As Congress was preparing to reconvene, President Reagan's speech writers were preparing another State of the Union address. The year before, the President's pull-at-your-heartstrings contrivance had been to show his commitment to education: a teacher would be the first civilian to go into space. Now, with the State of the Union address only a few days away, the space shuttle that would carry schoolteacher Christa McAuliffe into orbit was in its countdown. How dramatic it would be to have the teacher greet Congress from space during the President's speech!

On January 28, the shuttle exploded. The pictures were played over and over on the evening news. President Reagan delivered another eulogy to fallen heroes, and postponed his State of the Union address. A commission was formed to look into the *Challenger* disaster, and Richard was asked to be one of its members.

As February began, I remembered that the Silk Road exhibition had just opened in Göteborg. I telephoned Alan on a Sunday. "How about going up to Sweden and checking out the exhibition? You could meet Vainshtein, and see for yourself what the exhibition is like."

"I'll be glad to go," Alan said. "But why don't you go, too? A friend of a violist in the orchestra just flew from San Francisco to Brussels for $99 on People Express."

"Really? I wonder what the catch is—maybe it costs $999 to fly from Brussels to San Francisco."

I called People Express and found that on Wednesdays, to promote their new route, the nonstop flight from San Francisco to Brussels was indeed only $99 each way.

"What do I have to do to get a ticket—go down to the airport and camp out for two days?"

"No, I can make a reservation for you now, sir."

"You mean you still have seats available on these flights?"

"Yes we do, sir."

"Great! The names are Richard Feynman, Ralph Leighton, and Glen Cowan. We'll go to Brussels on February 6th and return to San Francisco on the 20th."

"Just purchase your tickets at a travel agency tomorrow, sir, and your place will be assured."

I phoned Alan. "I'm coming!" I also phoned Mats Jonson, the physicist I had visited in Göteborg, and asked whether he wouldn't mind being descended upon by a horde of Americans.

"You're always welcome," he said.

I also asked if he could arrange a meeting with the Soviets at the Göteborg Historical Museum.

I told the Chief about my plan, but he said he was going over to the Jet Propulsion Lab on Tuesday to learn about the shuttle, and would be in Washington beginning on Wednesday. "Why are you going to the exhibition in Sweden, man? You haven't done anything about bringing it to America since you came back last summer. I think you're a little nutty on this one."

"I know," I said. "I wasn't going to go, but this fare I can't pass up—and our lodging in Sweden is free. I won't make any promises to the Soviets; I'd just like to see the exhibition myself."

I called Glen. "What are you doing on Wednesday?"

"Just my regular routine," he replied. "Are you coming up to San Francisco?"

"Well, yeah," I said, "—on my way to Sweden."

"Sweden!?"

I explained the situation. Miraculously, Glen was willing to participate in this folly.

"I'll see you in three days," I said.

I telephoned Mats to find out about meeting the Soviets.

"You know, it's an amusing coincidence," he said. "I contacted the Museum and found out that the man in charge of the exhibition is someone I see nearly every week—our daughters have ballet class together. He'll be happy to arrange a meeting with the Soviets when you come."

"Great. I'll call you from Bochum when I know which train we'll be on. Thanks!"

On Wednesday morning I flew to San Francisco and met Glen at the airport. During the comfortable flight to Brussels, Glen spent several hours listening to tapes from a Swedish language course he had taken for a year at UCLA, occasionally blurting out a phrase that, because of its melodic intonation, sounded more like Chinese than a European language.

By Thursday night we reached Bochum, where Alan and Linda met us and drove us to their apartment. The next day we drove to Düsseldorf to pick up some T-shirts that Alan and Linda, a graphic artist, had designed. One shirt said "ТЫВА" ("Tuva" in Cyrillic Tuvan) in the shape of a map of Tuva; the others were white with black lettering and a red heart: "кызылга ♥ мен."

"Where did you find out how to say 'Kyzyl love I' in Tuvan?" I asked.

"I phoned Professor Krueger," said Alan. "His payment will be some 'I ♥ Copenhagen' stickers that we'll pick up on the way back from Sweden."

Late that night we took the train to Copenhagen and transferred to a train bound for Helsingør (Elsinore), where we boarded a ferry for the five-mile trip to Sweden. The harbor was covered with large sheets of ice. The Southern Californians debated whether the ice floes were made only from frozen freshwater (that is, rain and snow hitting very cold saltwater), or from frozen saltwater as well.

We boarded a Swedish train and arrived in Göteborg that afternoon. Mats and his four-year-old daughter Emma met us at the train station and said we were going directly to the Göteborg Historical Museum.

"But look at us," I said. "Our clothes are rumpled from the night on the train, and my brother and I are unshaven."

"It doesn't matter," Mats said. "The Soviets are very eager to see you."

We entered the Museum through a side door and ascended to the second floor, where the director, Christian Axel-Nilsson, had his office. A hearty man with a ruddy complexion, Axel-Nilsson welcomed us to his museum with a bottle of sherry. He introduced the Museum's ethnographer, Dr. Silow—the man Mats knew from his daughter's ballet class.

Glen bowled everyone over with his impeccable Swedish. After a few minutes of small talk, the door behind us opened to reveal the Soviet director of the exhibition. I had seen this handsome man before, in Vainshtein's apartment. "Greetings, Ralph Leighton," he said, clicking his heels and bowing as he extended his hand. "It is a pleasure to meet you again."

"Uh, hello, uh—"

"Dr. Basilov," said Glen, in the nick of time.

"Greetings, Glen Cowan," said Dr. Basilov, with charm oozing from every pore.

Glen answered him with some pleasant words in Russian.

As further pleasantries were exchanged, I couldn't avoid being impressed by the VIP reception that we—a ragtag bunch of unwashed, uncultured Americans—were being accorded by the refined, civilized Swedes and their Russian counterparts.

As little Emma ate cheese puffs and stood on her head, we began to discuss which American museums would be appropriate for the exhibition. Axel-Nilsson thought the Smithsonian Institution would be the best place to start. Dr. Basilov hesitated, noting that the Smithsonian was already preparing to host a joint Soviet-American exhibition called "Crossroads," which featured the native cultures on both sides of the Bering Strait.

After more conversation and another round of sherry, there was a knock on the same door behind us. It was Sevyan Vainshtein. Although the delayed entrance by Vainshtein had heightened my sense of anticipation, Glen interpreted it as a move designed by Basilov to show Vainshtein's inferior rank.

Vainshtein offered to show us around the exhibition, so we accompanied him. Hundreds of people crowded around the austere, white museum cases full of artifacts made of gold, silver, bronze, copper, and even wood, leather, and cloth. (Ice in the frozen earth of Siberia and Mongolia preserved those otherwise perishable materials.) Vainshtein concentrated on the considerable number of items he had personally excavated in Tuva. One of them was a golden object from the Scythian period (800–200 B.C.) portraying a wild boar biting a hunter, whose dog was biting the boar.

"Wow!" I exclaimed. "I've read about this one!" I told everyone about the little article Richard had found in the *Los Angeles Times* eight years before, describing the sculpture. I took a picture of it for the Chief.

Vainshtein then showed us other impressive artifacts from Tuva: the big bronze plaque of a coiled panther that was featured in his book on Tuvan art; from the Hunnic period (A.D. 1–500), arrows with holes in their odd-shaped tips, causing them to whistle in flight; and from the ancient Turkic period (A.D. 550–1200), a life-sized "stone man"—similar to one I had seen in Mächen-Helfen's book—standing in the middle of the hall.

Despite Vainshtein's emphasis on things Tuvan, I couldn't help noticing the dazzling reconstruction of a costume called the "Golden Man," found in the grave of a nobleman from Scythian times who had lived in what today is Kazakhstan. The original gold pieces, now too fragile to display as a costume, were housed in a nearby case. They were impressive examples of the Scythian "animal style" of art. Horses, moose, and stags with stylized antlers all conveyed a sense of action and power. The Golden Man's two-foot-tall headdress sported arrows pointing skyward, a winged mythical beast with two heads, and a pair of snarling snow leopards.

After our tour I asked Mats if we could have further discussions with the Soviets at his house. Mats suggested dinner that evening. Vainshtein accepted, but when we found Basilov he politely declined, citing "other engagements."

We shook hands with everyone and departed with Mats and Emma. Mats broke the news to his wife, Elizabeth, that Vainshtein might also be coming over that evening. "But

In 1982 Richard read that a Scythian gold sculpture—showing a dog (head visible at right) biting a boar (center), which is biting a hunter (bent over at top)—was discovered in Tuva. In 1986 it came to Sweden as part of the exhibition *On the Silk Road.* (Courtesy Aurora Publishers, Leningrad.)

probably not," he said. "Dr. Silow said that the Russians often do not show up, after saying they will come."

When dinnertime approached, Glen and I went with Mats to the Three Crowns Hotel to look for Vainshtein. He wasn't hard to find: he was standing at the entrance, along with two other Russians! "Is it all right if they come along too?" he asked. Mats could only accept.

We all squeezed into mat's VW Dasher and returned home. Elizabeth seemed unfazed by the additional influx of guests.

Vainshtein's two Soviet colleagues spoke only Russian. Vadim Kurylov, an ethnographer from Leningrad, looked like Leo Tolstoy's older brother; Vladimir Lamin, a historian from Novosibirsk, looked like Andrei Gromyko's younger brother.

Elizabeth had prepared "Swedish pizza": the crust was fillo dough, and the toppings were Swedish cheeses, sausages, and peppers—a real treat to the eyes as well as the palate. The Soviets had brought some Armenian cognac, and began their customary toasts. As in Moscow, Vainshtein gave a lengthy salute to Richard Feynman. He regretted once again not being able to meet Richard, and remarked that he felt a certain attraction to him—something like the pull of gravity. He proposed, therefore, that the laws of gravitation be revised to take into account the "Feynman effect." Glen gave a toast in Swedish to Mats's wife for preparing such a fine dinner; I gave a toast in honor of *Shagaa*, the Tuvan New Year, which happened to be that night.

In the flickering candlelight of the Jonsons' dining room, Glen translated as Vainshtein recounted a Tuvan adventure: he and his colleagues were excavating the Uighur fortress on the island in Lake Tere-Khol when a fisherman came by and asked if they would like to meet a shaman. They gladly took a break from their work and—as in mythic tales—went with the fisherman in his boat across the lake to another world.

The visitors came upon a yurt and found the shaman, whose name was Shonchur, along with his wife and brother. Vainshtein asked Shonchur how he had become a shaman.

Shonchur replied that when he was fourteen years old he became ill and ran into the forest. When he returned, he still had not recovered; in fact, he was even more sick—he could hardly walk. When his parents asked what had happened to him, Shonchur couldn't remember anything. So they called in the local shaman to see what could be done about their son's strange illness.

The shaman said young Shonchur had received the spirit of his grandfather [presumably a shaman], a sign that Shonchur should become a shaman himself.

Shonchur didn't want to become a shaman, but was told he had no choice after such an illness. So he served many years as an intermediary to the spirit world while herding reindeer in eastern Tuva, during which time he got married.

When his first wife died, Shonchur visited his brother at Lake Tere-Khol and met a woman there who was a cattle herder. He married her and settled down in his brother's village, where he continued to practice shamanism. He eventually became an "Ulug Kham," a great shaman.

Vainshtein asked him to perform a ceremony. Shonchur said they must wait until dark. In the meantime Vainshtein helped Shonchur put on his costume—a feathered headdress, some leather trousers, and a cape with numerous iron pendants that represented helping spirits and various parts of the body—which weighed about fifty pounds. One of Vainshtein's colleagues snapped the photo that ended up on the back jacket of *Nomads of South Siberia*. (See pp. 50–51.)

When evening came, Shonchur made a fire inside the yurt to dry out his drum. [I thought of my friend Thomas Rutishauser, who would tighten the heads on his Mexican bongos by holding them over a candle flame.] To reach the spirit world faster, Shonchur threw a local narcotic grass into the fire and breathed its aromatic smoke. He also sprinkled some milk into the fire to feed his "horse." Shonchur, like most Siberian shamans, regarded his drum as a horse and the drumstick as a whip.

Still inside the yurt, Shonchur turned his back to Vainshtein and the others and sat down. He tapped his drum lightly and started to mumble softly. Even after his mumbling changed into words, they were difficult to understand—they were archaic Tuvan—but gradually the idea became clear: the shaman was summoning his guardian spirit and his helping spirits.

At first Shonchur moved only a little. As he beat the drum louder, he moved more and more, until his feathered headdress slipped down over his face. The shaman was in a trance.

After more rhythmic beating of his "horse," Shonchur reached a state of ecstasy. His face was covered with sweat; he was unpleasant to look at. He ran around inside the yurt, beating his drum, flushing out evil spirits. He chased the spirits outside, yelling at them while beating his drum.

Shonchur set about corralling the evil spirits into his drum. Occasionally one would pop out, whereupon he would jump on it and wrestle with it, crying, "I'm going to kill you and tear open your arteries and drink your blood!"

After rounding up all the evil spirits and destroying them, Shonchur staggered back into his yurt and collapsed. Vainshtein was afraid he had died. But after a few long moments the shaman opened his eyes and smiled. Vainshtein helped him take off his heavy costume. Shonchur said age was taking its toll, so Vainshtein arranged for him to see a doctor. The last great shaman of Tuva died a few years later.

After dinner, conversation continued in the Jonsons' living room. Vainshtein began talking about Feynman again and then asked me point-blank why he had not visited the USSR before, especially in view of the widespread acclaim there for *The Feynman Lectures on Physics.* Richard had told

me the reason before: "I don't like the way the Russian government treats its people—especially its scientists." It was not
only Dr. Sakharov, at that time on a hunger strike, whom
Richard was concerned about; he knew that Soviet scientists
could not work without interference from the Communist
Party. He quoted Thomas Jefferson: "I have sworn upon the
altar of God eternal hostility against every form of tyranny
over the mind of man."

I didn't have the nerve (or the ability in German) to say all
that to Vainshtein, who seemed perfectly satisfied with life in
the USSR, so I gave an additional reason: "Because he won
the Nobel prize, everyone would follow him around," I said.
"Professor Feynman wants to visit Tuva incognito."

Vainshtein understood, and replied that it was the same
with the King of Sweden coming to see the Silk Road exhibition in Göteborg—he wanted to visit as an ordinary citizen,
with no fanfare. (That was just about possible in a country
where the Prime Minister routinely went to the theater as an
ordinary citizen, without security guards.)

As discussions continued, I decided to play show and tell. I
began with my TOUVA license plate, which I had temporarily taken off my car. Vainshtein explained to the other Soviets
how he had discovered our picture in *Tuvinskaya Pravda*.

I had also brought along my satellite photo of Tuva.
Vainshtein was agog. I assured him that anyone could order
Landsat photos from the government. "Here," I said. "You
can keep it if you wish." He accepted it with amazement and
sincere appreciation.

As the evening drew to a close, the Soviets brought out a
porcelain tea set from Moscow and presented it to Elizabeth.
She placed it in a display cabinet, in a spot that suddenly had
seemed empty before. The Soviets were pleased that their gift
had found such a good home.

To finish off the evening, Alan brought down some of the
"Kyzyl ♥ I" T-shirts that he and Linda had designed and

presented them to everyone. As the rest of us collapsed into bed, Mats delivered the Soviets back to their hotel.

On Monday morning Alan and Linda left for Bochum by train. Because it was the beginning of a one-week winter school vacation, the Jonsons went out of town to visit Elizabeth's mother for a few days. Glen and I took the tram downtown and met with the Soviets in their "yurt," an office set aside for them on the third floor of the museum. The air was thick with the distinctive smoke of Soviet cigarettes. Dr. Basilov welcomed us with his characteristic bow, presented us with a book on Islamic shamanism he had written, and offered us some Georgian tea which Kurylov had prepared.

Basilov immediately launched into a list of enterprising ideas about how the exhibition could be marketed to the American public. His first idea was to sell kumiss, the fermented mare's milk brew that was central to a Eurasian nomad's diet. "And of course, we should bring some Kazakh milkmaids over to milk the horses," he said.

We smiled and said, "Why not?"

Basilov then enlarged on his idea: "We should also bring some yurts to set up in front of the museum—they cost only two thousand rubles each—and have some Kazakh and Turkmenian women pounding felt and weaving rugs nearby, which they could sell to the public."

"Sounds good to me," I said.

"We could bring some camels along, too, since they are also used by the nomads, and offer rides to the children—for a small fee, of course. And we could have Uzbek women preparing *plov* [pilaf], as well as their special bread." Basilov was so proud of himself for thinking of all these money-making ideas that he joked to his Soviet colleagues that he should become a capitalist.

Vainshtein asked us what we thought about the exhibition.

Glen praised it thoroughly, but that didn't bring the expected satisfaction from our hosts.

I decided to say exactly what was on my mind. "I think the title 'Silk Road' is misleading: it conjures up images of Marco Polo and China, whereas the exhibition really seems to be about the nomads who lived to the north of the Silk Road."

Basilov seemed pleased. "As you may know, in Russian the exhibition is called 'Nomads of Eurasia.' Why can't we use that title? Does it sound too academic?"

"The 'Nomads' part is good," I said. "Especially in California, where we like the idea of always being on the move. There used to be an automobile called the Chevy Nomad—it was a favorite among the surfers."

"In Japan, all they wanted to see was gold," Basilov complained. "Much more significant to the life of the nomads were 'dull' things like the saddle and the stirrup."

"Californians love horses," I said. "Perhaps the catalog cover could show the side of a horse, with a horseman's foot in a stirrup."

"Wunderbar!" exclaimed Vainshtein, who had written an article with a colleague about the origin of stirrups.[1]

Basilov then explained the bureaucracy to us: "The chairman of the USSR Academy of Sciences is Academician A. P. Alexandrov, and the official in charge of exhibitions is Corresponding Member A. P. Kapitsa. The first step is for an appropriate counterpart in the United States to write a letter to Academician Alexandrov—with an official copy to Kapitsa and an unofficial copy to me. Then, when I receive my copy, I can nudge Kapitsa to tap Alexandrov."

I winked at Glen, who had already caught the significance

[1]In the article ("Sedlo i stremya" ["The Saddle and the Stirrup"], *Sovetskaya Etnografiya*, Vol. 6, 1984, pp. 114–130), Vainshtein and M. V. Kryukov cited archaeological evidence showing that the first use of the stirrup—usually found only on the left side—was to assist in mounting a horse.

of Basilov's words: the Friends of Tuva now had a mole, deep inside the USSR Academy of Sciences!

Basilov then suggested some organizations and personalities who might be an appropriate counterpart to the USSR Academy of Sciences. "Your National Academy of Sciences, of course—or perhaps your famous senator, Ted Kennedy."

We weren't excited about either suggestion, since we didn't have any contacts on the East Coast.

Basilov continued: "There is an institute in California—the Esalen Institute. Have you heard of it?"

"Yes, we've heard of it," said Glen, smiling broadly.

I was about to mention the nudes bathing in the scenic hot pools when I remembered the contingent at Esalen—a low-key group led by co-founder Michael Murphey—that was working to improve relations with the Soviet Union. Their most famous project was the "space bridge" that linked the two sides by satellite.[2] So I said, "In fact, Professor Feynman has given seminars there."

Vainshtein suggested that Feynman himself was an appropriate counterpart to Academician Alexandrov. Glen and I heartily agreed. Basilov wasn't so sure, but reluctantly went along with the idea.

Basilov warned us that Alexandrov was in poor health, and that Feynman should write him right away, before the Academy got bogged down choosing his successor. I replied that our Chief was serving on the presidential commission investigating the space shuttle *Challenger* disaster, but was confident he could find time for matters relating to Tuva.

It was time for lunch. The Soviets offered us bread—brought from the USSR, it appeared—along with kasha garnished with canned horse meat. Glen immediately became a

[2]Later, in 1989, the Esalen Institute brought Boris Yeltsin to the United States. During his stay he met with President Bush and leaders of Congress.

vegetarian. We washed down our rations with generous amounts of Georgian tea.

In the afternoon we all worked together to draft the letter from Feynman to Alexandrov. Basilov suggested certain phrases to make the Academy of Sciences more receptive—he called it "playing the Soviet tune." Glen knew the melody by heart, having succeeded in getting our picture into *Tuvinskaya Pravda* by the same kind of formulistic writing. By the time we were finished, the letter went like this:

Dear Chairman Alexandrov,

I am writing you in connection with the recent exhibition arranged by the USSR Academy of Sciences called "On the Silk Road." It is by way of my interest in the remote region of Southern Siberia called Tuva that I found out about it.

I agree with your sentiments, expressed in the foreword of the exhibition catalog, that the advance of culture comes about more rapidly by increased exchanges of ideas, and thus the role of the Eurasian nomadic peoples has been of immense historical significance. For the same reason, I hope the exhibition "On the Silk Road" can come to the United States.

Two friends of mine, Ralph Leighton and Glen Cowan, temporarily assumed the role of nomads and traveled to Sweden to see the exhibition. (Unfortunately, I was unable to go myself.) At the exhibition, Mr. Leighton and Mr. Cowan met with Soviet experts. From reports of their discussions, I am confident that the exhibition can be presented here with great success, resulting in a better understanding by people in the United States of the great diversity of cultures in the USSR and of Soviet scholarship in that area.

I therefore ask for your support and cooperation in arranging for the exhibition "On the Silk Road" to come to the United States. Assuming that you have no objections, Mr. Leighton, Mr. Cowan, and I are contacting appropriate orga-

nizations and museums in the United States that could host
the exhibition here.

> Sincerely,
> Richard Feynman

Our "negotiations" had gone so well that the Soviets invited us to their hotel that evening for dinner. "It is time for
the Soviet side to entertain the American side," said Basilov,
in calculated diplomatic language.

"The American side accepts with pleasure," replied Glen
with equal finesse. We all shook hands and parted with smiles
all around.

Before we left the Museum we dropped in on Axel-Nilsson.
He offered to meet us in his office at 9 A.M. the following day
to discuss the exhibition.

As we made our way back to Mats's home, we were eu-
phoric. "Wow!" I said. "We're real diplomats now!" Speaking
to an imaginary diplomatic press corps, I said, "The negotiations between the Soviet and American sides have been conducted in an atmosphere of friendship and mutual respect."
We both laughed. We felt as if we had worked out the details
of a treaty for Gorbachev and Reagan.

Glen smiled. "Axel-Nilsson must wonder why the Soviets
are wasting their time on a couple of clowns from California—I mean, if they want to bring their exhibition to the
United States, why don't *they* write a letter to the National
Academy of Sciences, or Ted Kennedy . . ."

"Or Esalen," I said, and we both laughed some more.

"Maybe the USSR Academy of Sciences is no different
from Mir publishers or that ice cream parlor in Tbilisi," I
said. "If a Soviet wants something, he's ignored. If a foreigner
wants something, he's served right away."

"It's the Soviets' loss and our gain," replied Glen. "A trio of amateurs trying to get to Tuva end up negotiating cultural relations between the superpowers."

"The Chief is gonna love it!" I exclaimed. "The professor of physics is about to become a big cheese in the world of international exhibitions!"

Clowns or Con Men?

9 AFTER several hours of rest at Mats's house, we walked to the Three Crowns Hotel to meet the Soviets for dinner. We went to the room of Vainshtein, who then took us around to find the other Soviets.

The hotel seemed empty except for the four Russians. We knew it wasn't exactly high tourist season in Göteborg, but this was below low season—it was dead. The "Soviet side"—Basilov, Vainshtein, Kurylov, and Lamin—led us to the desolate dining room.

The waiter greeted us with a courteous "Dobryi vyecher," but did not bring a menu. Basilov was not offended; he pulled out six coupons and handed them over. Lamin pulled out a small bottle of vodka from his coat, and the waiter provided shot glasses.

Soon the waiter returned with our meal, chicken with rice pilaf. Every plate was identical.

During dinner we talked about life in the

United States and the Soviet Union. Basilov described the Lenin library in Moscow, the largest in the USSR. "No one is allowed into the stacks. Once the book is retrieved for you, you may not take it home—you must look at it in the library."

"That's just like our Library of Congress," I said. "Except that you can borrow the book later through your local library on an inter-library loan."

Glen described the Doe research library at Berkeley, one of the world's largest. "Professors and graduate students are allowed into the stacks; undergraduates and the general public have to request a book by filling out a card. University students and faculty can borrow books for a few weeks or even a few months, but the general public can't—they must read the books inside the library."

"Doesn't that lead to the problem of missing pages?" Basilov asked.

I didn't understand. Glen caught on and said, "We only have that problem at public telephone booths—usually it's the motel or restaurant pages that are missing. As in most libraries, there are Xerox machines if you need to copy something."

I had read that Xerox machines were practically nonexistent in the USSR: the rulers feared that independent—that is, subversive—ideas would be widely circulated if copy machines were generally available.

"Our problem is much more serious," said Basilov. "I am a scholar. I need to do my research. But when I finally obtain permission to look at an important book, I discover that some critical pages have been torn out by some bloody bastard who was too lazy to write down the information for himself." Basilov's face was tense. "Such criminals should be flogged in public—by the librarians!"

Eventually the conversation turned to Tuva. Glen explained to Lamin and Kurylov how we had tried for so long to get to Kyzyl. Vainshtein was silent as to why the Institute of

Ethnography in Moscow had not been able to arrange our visit. Basilov, also uncharacteristically quiet, plowed through his dinner like a bulldozer.

As we finally caught up to him, Basilov asked Glen and me whether we liked the food.

"Certainly," we replied.

"So, then, let us enjoy the pleasure again," said Basilov, whereupon he pulled out six more coupons from his coat. The waiter said the cook had made only enough rice for six dinners, so we would have to wait twenty minutes. By Soviet standards, that was fast—only twice the time it took a typical waiter to come over to your table and tell you it's not in service.

As we waited for dinner number two, the normally taciturn Lamin explained something to me in Russian. Glen translated: "Lamin says he can invite either one of us to Novosibirsk—or both of us, if we're married to each other (ha, ha)—and from there he can arrange a trip to Tuva."

I asked Glen to tell Lamin, "Your invitation is very generous, but like the Three Musketeers—you know, 'all for one and one for all'—Professor Feynman, Glen, and I are determined to reach Tuva together."

After our second dinner the Soviets invited us upstairs for tea. Lamin dispensed with his suit and donned a white T-shirt and a pair of well-worn Levis. We met in Basilov's room, which was presumably the largest.

As Kurylov prepared tea, Basilov told several "Georgian jokes." These ethnic jokes, instead of denigrating their target, were told with a certain admiration and envy. Apparently Georgian men have a reputation for sexual prowess—especially when compared to Russian men. (Russian women on factory vacations at Red Riviera resorts often seek sexual adventure with local Georgian men. And when Georgian men go to other areas of the USSR as summer laborers, local women bored with life and looking for a good time readily lend themselves to the virile visitors.)

A sample Georgian joke: a beautiful young woman from France descends from the airplane on a visit to Georgia. She cannot evade the long line of Georgian men leering at her, so she looks at one of them and says, innocently, "Parlez-vous français?"

"Of course I want to!" says the man in his native Georgian, to the cheers of his fellow countrymen.

Since our relations had now ascended to such a high level of mutual trust, I told Basilov about Esalen—the hot pools, the massage tables, the alternative paths to enlightenment that people seek there. I said, "People pay to hear about things like shamanism—not as an academic discipline, but as a belief system capable of healing them of their ailments and their spiritual maladies. In fact, you could lead a seminar at Esalen, telling stories about how shamans have healed the sick in Central Asia. I guarantee you'll have more women (and men) at your feet than you know what to do with!"

Basilov replied, "Perhaps in modern society, where the standard sources of power and authority are crumbling, people turn to more primitive traditions for spiritual fulfillment."

I laughed. "You got it!"

"A few years ago I was invited to the Esalen Institute," Basilov said ruefully, "but someone crossed my path and prevented me from accepting this invitation. What a pity!"

I replied, "If the exhibition comes to Los Angeles, I'll find a way for you to visit the place."

It was getting late. Glen and I bade the Soviets goodnight and walked back to Mats's house under a starry sky. As we got ready for bed, Glen thought of our meeting with Axel-Nilsson in the morning: "What are we going to ask him?"

"I have no idea," I replied. "I'm too tired to think of anything now. Maybe something will come to me in my sleep."

At what seemed like an hour later, my alarm clock went off. It was pitch black outside, but it was 8 A.M. We hurriedly ate some bread and cheese and made our way to the tram stop in the late morning dawn. As we rode into the center of town, Glen asked me if I had thought of anything to ask Axel-Nilsson.

"Not yet," I replied. "I guess our best hope is to get him talking so he answers his own questions."

"I'm really nervous," said Glen. "We're about to be exposed for what Axel-Nilsson has always thought we are—a couple of clowns from California."

"I know what you mean," I replied. "I feel like everything is about to unravel. My mind is blank right now—the past few days have been too intense!"

We reached the Museum just before 9 A.M. Axel-Nilsson invited us into his office. "Would you like some coffee?" he asked.

We engaged in some small talk. Axel-Nilsson said he admired how a couple of Californians had the courage—perhaps due to a lack of social class constraints—to deal with the Soviets without a proper introduction. Having seen the exhibition in Finland, he had been introduced to the Soviets by a Finn who had extensive contacts with the USSR Academy of Sciences.

Then Axel-Nilsson's face suddenly became stern. He took on a serious countenance, squinting with one eye, and leaned forward. He said, "The first thing you should know about this exhibition is that the archaeological material in it is *extraordinary*. For example, the Hunnic riding pants excavated in Mongolia are nearly two thousand years old. They are extremely fragile. If we had such things in Sweden, we would never let them out of the country!"

Before we knew it Axel-Nilsson was recounting who his contacts in Finland and the USSR were, who in the Soviet delegation liked to drink and what the favorite liquor was, how the protocol was negotiated, how much the exhibition should be insured for, how it was crated in Leningrad and transported by truck through Finland into Sweden, how much was paid to the visiting Soviets per diem, how he had to give the Soviets meal coupons because he was concerned for their health (Soviets tend to save every bit of hard currency for consumer goods to take home), and so on, and so on, and so on—he laid out the exhibition business in detail for two hours!

Finally, Axel-Nilsson had a question for us: "Why are you doing this?"

I could think of nothing but to tell him the truth—our fascination for Tuva, how Feynman had corresponded with Vainshtein, and how Glen and I found out about the exhibition in Vainshtein's apartment. "Right now our plan is to find a museum in the United States to host the exhibition. Then we'll visit Tuva as members of that museum," I said.

"That's interesting," Axel-Nilsson replied. "My passion is typefaces. One of the best Gothic collections is here in Sweden, because nearly all the Gothic type in Germany was melted down during the war. But the Smithsonian has an even better collection—one of the world's best. In fact, I would appreciate it if you could mention my name to the person in charge of the typeface collections when you talk with the Smithsonian about bringing the exhibition there."

I strained to keep a straight face as I imagined Richard's delight at the prospect of some clowns from California providing the Swedish museum director an entrée to the Smithsonian.

It was time for lunch. We walked over to a nearby restaurant through the cold but invigorating wind, and continued our conversations. Matters became personal: Axel-Nilsson had been brought in to rescue the ailing Göteborg Historical Museum; the exhibition was a way to raise public interest and government money. He discussed his health problems (lower back pain) as well as his happy family life. He invited us to join the Soviets for supper at his apartment later that week and meet his wife and children.

When we returned to the Museum, Axel-Nilsson filled us with more information. I wrote notes as fast as I could, but I could hardly think. I felt like a spacecraft acquiring mountains of data as it flew past a planet—the information would have to be analyzed and digested later.

Axel-Nilsson made copies of the protocol between the Göteborg Historical Museum and the USSR Academy of Sciences for us to take home to Los Angeles. He also made copies of all the business cards he had picked up in the course of arranging the exhibition, and finally loaded us down with a dozen catalogs. By the time he was through, he had even offered to make the Swedish diplomatic pouch available to us for communication with Moscow!

By now it was 4 P.M. We thanked Axel-Nilsson for all his help and trundled off with our papers and catalogs in plastic bags specially made for the exhibition.

We walked through the center of town in a daze. We hardly spoke to each other—there was just too much information swirling in our heads.

Finally, I said, "Uh, Glen: this is a strange thought, and I don't want you to misunderstand me. But from all the details that Axel-Nilsson gave us about the exhibition—how to arrange for it, how it is transported, and so on—if we were con men, we could pull off one of the robberies of the century!"

"I was thinking the same thing," said Glen. "But we probably don't know how good the cops are." (In fact, we didn't know how good the Göteborg Historical Museum was: it had run a background check on us already!)

When we got to Mats's house, I telephoned Phoebe Kwan in Pasadena—Phoebe was now my fiancée—to tell her of our great progress, and asked her to relay the news to the Chief, who was in Washington on the Rogers Commission. I also called Christopher Sykes in London. Sykes had produced a masterful interview with Richard called "The Pleasure of Finding Things Out," which had aired on "Nova" a few years before. He knew about our fascination for Tuva, and was thinking of making a film about it. "The exhibition is great," I said. "And we're in the thick of negotiations with the Soviets and the Swedes. You oughta come over and see it for yourself."

Sykes replied, "Unfortunately, I'm tied up in London, but I'll be coming out to Los Angeleez in about ten days."

"Then I'll tell you all about it at the Feynmans'," I replied, once again inviting a guest to someone else's home.

We switched on the television and watched the evening news. There was a report from Washington, D.C., about the space shuttle inquiry. The reporter was standing on the steps in front of the Capitol. "Föne upp doh Naazaa ette själling pukko Richard Feynman ek tunnet . . ." and suddenly there was the Chief, holding a little C-clamp in his hand, explaining something. For us, it was icing on the cake: the third musketeer of the Tuva trio had suddenly appeared in Sweden after all.

The next morning Phoebe called back and said that the Chief wanted some catalogs right away. She gave me his telephone number in Washington, and said to call him at 6:30 A.M. Washington time.

At the Museum Axel-Nilsson's secretary got in touch with an air courier service and sent four catalogs. Then we went to see the Soviets in their smoky "yurt."

Vainshtein offered to show us his slides of Tuva. To reach the room where the projector was located, we had to walk for about thirty seconds outside, across a courtyard. Vainshtein bundled himself up completely—overcoat, scarf, and gloves. Glen and I figured that thirty seconds outside wouldn't kill us, even if we were wearing only T-shirts. But from the way Vainshtein warned us to wrap ourselves up, we could see that just looking at us made him cold. We wondered how he had ever survived a winter in Tuva.

Vainshtein's slides were extremely dusty; the colors in some of them were beginning to change. But that didn't take away from their exciting content, the stuff of postage stamps.

Just before 12:30 we interrupted the slide show to telephone Richard from Axel-Nilsson's office. "Hey, Chief!" I said. "How's Washington?"

"You know those jokes people make about how crazy Washington is? Well, they don't even begin to describe it."

I laughed. "Chief, Glen and I saw you on Swedish TV last night. You were the main news from Washington, can you believe it? It was great to see you. What were you doing with the C-clamp?"

"Oh, I just did a little experiment with some rubber from the rocket. I dipped it in some ice water and showed that it's no good when it's cold." Little did I realize that Richard's "little experiment" had just blown the shuttle investigation wide open and would eventually transform the Rogers Commission from a rubber-stamp body into a credible panel of investigators.

"Chief, I've got someone here who is dying to talk to you." I handed the telephone to Vainshtein.

"Grüsse Professor Feynman. Wie geht es Ihnen?"

Feynman said something back. Vainshtein was in heaven. As the two Jewish gentlemen conversed, I marveled that the Chief could hold his own in German for so long with no warning at 6:30 in the morning.

When I got the telephone back I said, "Hey, Chief, I hear you wanted some catalogs. The museum just sent you four by air courier."

"That's fine," said Richard. "There's a fella named Acheson[1] on the commission. He happens to be on the Smithsonian's board of directors."

"Wow! You're really going right to work!"

"That's right, man!"

"Oh, yeah: Chris Sykes will be in California in about ten days."

"Just say when, and I'll tell the commission that I have to be back in Pasadena for something really important," said Richard. "Tuva or bust!"

I smiled. "Tuva or bust! Good luck, Chief, and so long for now!"

We went back to finish the slide show. Tuva was everything we had dreamed of, and more. We couldn't wait to go. The last photo was of Vainshtein and his wife at the "Centre of Asia" monument in Kyzyl holding up a sign. It said in Russian, "Greetings, Richard Feynman!"

"Please take this picture to Professor Feynman," said Sevyan. "And this one, too." It was a photo of the Vainshteins holding the same sign beside a yurt.

Glen and I accompanied Sevyan back through the courtyard to the Soviets' "yurt," where Tuva talk continued. As the others sipped tea, Vainshtein addressed me with the informal *du* in German: "Ralph, you and I should write a popular book together about Tuva, with Glen as translator."

"That's a great idea!" I replied. "Feynman could be the photographer." I knew that the Chief would learn all about photography to prepare for the trip. Long experienced in drawing, he was already an accomplished artist.

"You must find a publisher in the USA to contact our agency, VAAP," Vainshtein counseled. "VAAP will then contact me and ask whether I am interested in writing a book with you about Tuva. I will take the matter under consideration for a few days and then, of course, say yes."

---

[1]David Acheson, a prominent Washington lawyer.

Sevyan Vainshtein, his wife, and a Tuvan colleague send greetings from Tuva's monument to the center of Asia, our holy grail. (Courtesy Sevyan Vainshtein.)

"I'll see what I can do," I said. "In the meantime, we should outline the book together while I am here in Sweden, so I can show the publisher something when I go back to the States."

"Let's do it tomorrow morning," Vainshtein suggested.

"Fine. I'll make an outline of my own tonight."

Then I brought up another idea, with Christopher Sykes in mind. "I think the exhibition would be more interesting if there were some video material to accompany it," I said. "We have a friend who makes films for the BBC. Perhaps he could go to Tuva with us and film some archaeological sites."

Basilov joined the conversation and said, "Such video material would be very useful and interesting. But I have one piece of advice: your friend must not come as a representative of the BBC. Otherwise, Soviet TV will become involved, and they will send representatives with you everywhere you go. It is better that your friend comes as a member of your museum delegation. In that way, the whole matter can be handled by the Soviet Academy of Sciences under the protocol."

As Glen and I prepared to leave, I assured Vainshtein and Basilov that both ideas should be pursued simultaneously. "After all, we have tried so many ways to get to Tuva—and so far, all have failed!"

On Thursday morning I went to the Museum to compare notes with Vainshtein, while Glen relaxed at Mats's house. Our outlines on Tuva were remarkably similar, to my relief. The only significant difference was that Vainshtein proposed a preface called "Let's Get Acquainted," in which he would introduce himself and tell how he became interested in Tuva: like Richard, Sevyan had collected stamps as a boy; years later he, too, wondered, "What ever happened to Tannu Tuva?" After completing his studies in ethnography (after briefly studying physics), Vainshtein had a choice: to be a small fish in a big pond (a staff member at a museum in Moscow or Kiev), or a big fish in a small pond (the director of a museum in Kyzyl). He chose to begin his career in the land of his

Sevyan Vainshtein and his wife, Alla, standing outside our dream hotel in Tuva. (Courtesy Sevyan Vainshtein.)

childhood stamp collection—which had just been accepted into the fraternity of nationalities called the Soviet Union.

Of course, any prospective publisher of a popular book on Tuva would want to see photographs, and in Göteborg—home of Hasselblad cameras—there was ample opportunity to get Vainshtein's captivating slides copied. But I never thought to do it.

We hadn't worked our way through the outline before Vainshtein had to excuse himself to join a lunch and shopping expedition arranged by a local town committee for the Soviets. He invited me to return to the Museum at 6 P.M. so we could go together to the supper that Axel-Nilsson was having at his home for the "visiting Soviet and American delegations."

Unfortunately, Glen could not go to the Axel-Nilsson's that evening (it was the only night a gorgeous cousin—distantly related—could have him over for dinner), so I went on my own to the Museum at the appointed hour to meet the Soviets. I had dressed light (one layer of pants, one layer of socks, and some dress shoes that didn't fit right), figuring that we would take a taxi or a tram to Axel-Nilsson's place. I was therefore surprised when Basilov took out a city map and led us for nearly an hour through the narrow streets of downtown Göteborg—always within earshot of the city trams, which were so cheap to ride that I offered to pay for everyone. The head of the "Soviet delegation" respectfully declined, citing the health benefits of walking.

When we reached Axel-Nilsson's home, Christian introduced us to his wife, Hélène, and to their two small children, whom Basilov adored and played with lovingly. Before we sat down to dinner, Vainshtein recounted one of the legends of Hodja Nasr Ad-Din Avanti, a wise man from medieval Central Asia: "A poor man, passing by a restaurant that was preparing pilaf with all the fixings, could only afford to eat bread. To 'augment' his meal he stood in the doorway of the restaurant, bit into his bread, and inhaled the luscious aromas of the pilaf."

"I've heard a similar story from my fiancée," I said. "A poor man in China could only afford to eat rice; to 'augment' his meal he breathed in the fragrant aromas wafting up from the kitchen."

"It is the same story," Vainshtein replied. "The greedy owner took the poor man before the mullah and demanded payment for the 'service' of augmenting the man's meal. The mullah decreed the poor man should pay—with the sounds of clinking coins."

The story was a perfect example of how the Silk Road was a conduit not only for goods but also for ideas and culture. Vainshtein remarked, "So the Silk Road extends to America."

"From both ends," I added, noting that I had heard one version of the story via China, and the other by way of Europe.

It was time for supper. We sat around a table in Axel-Nilsson's cozy kitchen. While the Muscovites and the American took only a small sip from their shot glasses in deference to Mikhail Gorbachev's recent initiative to curb alcoholism, the Siberian and the Swede drank their vodka the old-fashioned way: they quaffed it. The most dramatic toast was given by Axel-Nilsson himself. He raised his glass to Philip Johan von Strahlenberg, a Swede sent against his will to Siberia by Peter the Great in the early eighteenth century. Strahlenberg made the best of his unfortunate situation by studying the archaeology of southern Siberia, discovering inscriptions that reminded him of the Nordic runes of Scandinavia. "To Strahlenberg—and to no more political prisoners!" declared Axel-Nilsson with resolve.

The Soviets dutifully raised their glasses in silence.

After dinner we retired to the small living room packed with books and antiques. As the hour became late Axel-Nilsson was reluctant to drive us home—the drunk driving laws are strict in Sweden—so he called for a taxi. None was available for at least an hour. (They were busy driving other inebriated people home.) The trams had stopped running at midnight, so the only options left were to wait or to . . .

Basilov insisted that the "Soviet delegation" would enjoy walking the three miles back to their hotel: the night was quite warm by Russian standards—in the mid-twenties. Dressed more appropriately for the mid-twenties Celsius than Fahrenheit, I was nonetheless the "American delegation," so I couldn't wimp out.

We covered the distance to the Three Crowns Hotel in well under an hour. My frozen feet were oblivious to my ill-fitting shoes. I trotted the extra mile to Mats's house, where I sank into bed and tried to warm my frozen hands between my clammy knees.

Friday was our last day in Göteborg. In the late morning I finished going over the outline of the Tuva book with Vainshtein. Then I joined Glen for lunch, and in the afternoon we toured the Göteborg Historical Museum one last time. Basilov was scurrying around pasting up hastily typed captions next to the museum cases. "The Swedish public is so interested in this exhibition that they keep asking questions," he said.

We dropped in on Axel-Nilsson and thanked him for all his help. He offered to send us photographs of the museum cases showing the arrangement of the objects inside. We visited the Soviets' "yurt" and said goodbye to Lamin, Kurylov, and Vainshtein, who gave his regards once again to Feynman.

We returned by train to Bochum, where we reported the results of our "negotiations" to Alan and Linda. On Tuesday Glen and I explored Brugge, and on Wednesday we flew back to San Francisco on the $99 flight. By coincidence, the Chief had returned home the same day to take a break from Washington.

Chris Sykes was already in town. He and I went to the Feynmans' two days later for dinner, during which the Chief held forth on his experiences as a commissioner. He recounted how he had stayed a few days longer in Florida to talk to the engineers—to Chairman Rogers' disapproval—only to save the Chairman at a Senate hearing. "Senator Hollings was giving Mr. Rogers a hard time about his commission. The Senator said, 'The trouble with presidential commissions is, they go on what's *fed* to 'em, and they don't look behind it. . . . From my experience, I'd want four or five gumshoes going around down there at Canaveral talking to everybody, eating lunch with them. You'd be amazed, if you eat in the restaurants around there for two or three weeks, what you'll find out. You can't just sit and read what's given to you.' " The Chief continued, "Mr. Rogers was able to say, 'As a matter of fact, one of our commissioners is at Canaveral today, doing just that!' "

After dinner I covered the highlights of our trip to Sweden, and showed everyone the letter, drafted by the "Soviet and American sides" in Göteborg, that Richard was to send to Academician Alexandrov.

"This looks fine," said the Chief. "I'll take it to Caltech and have my secretary type it up and send it right away."

Then I took out a letter I had drafted to send to prospective host museums. Both Sykes and the Chief agreed that my style was too apologetic. "You're an expert, man!" said Richard. "You know more about this exhibition than anybody else in the country: you know all the people involved, how to arrange for it, how much it costs; you've got to have more confidence. You should rewrite the letter entirely."

We outlined the points of my new letter, and then dis-

cussed which museums to approach first. "Since I'm getting
to know Mr. Acheson, who's on the board of directors at the
Smithsonian, I'll handle that one," said the Chief.

"I'll start right here in Pasadena, with the Pacific Asia Museum," I replied.

After a few days of phone inquiries, I found out that the
Pacific Asia Museum had no money for such an ambitious
exhibition. Next on my list was the Los Angeles County Museum of Art.

"Is this the kind of art you can put on the wall?" the man
asked.

"No, it's artifacts."

"We rarely do that," he said. "The Natural History Museum would be more appropriate."

I called the Natural History Museum and eventually succeeded in setting up an appointment for the first week in
March.

On the last day of February, Sweden was suddenly thrust
into the news: Prime Minister Olaf Palme, leaving a theater
with his wife and walking in the street as an ordinary citizen,
without guards, was killed by a gunman who escaped into the
night. Although Glen and I had experienced plenty of excitement in Göteborg, we also had enjoyed a sense of peace and
detachment in that neutral Nordic country. Palme's assassination reminded me of November 22, 1963: in an instant a
nation lost its innocence.

On March 5 I went down to the Natural History Museum
and met Dr. Peter Keller, Associate Director for Public Programs, and Jim Olson, Chief of Exhibits. As they paged
through the Swedish catalog, I began to explain how it didn't
really capture the magnificence of the exhibition—but then I
caught myself: DON'T APOLOGIZE! SHOW CONFIDENCE!

Dr. Keller asked how much the participation fee was.

I had never heard of such a thing, but I guessed what it
might be. "There is no participation fee," I said calmly.

"None? You mean this exhibition is free?" Dr. Keller asked, incredulously.

I opened my manila folder. "Here's a copy of the protocol between the USSR and Sweden. There are some per diem costs you have to pay the Soviet specialists, but you don't have to pay anything directly to the museums or to the Academy of Sciences."

Keller and Olson had never heard of such an arrangement—but that didn't put them off.

"How much is your finder's fee?" asked Dr. Keller.

I had never heard of a finder's fee either, but I guessed what that might be, too. "Nothing," I said nonchalantly.

"Then what's in it for you?" asked Olson. "Why are you doing this?"

I tried to be as brief as I could with the Tuva story.

"I know exactly what you mean," said Olson. "My thing is Madagascar."

Dr. Keller asked, "How far is Tuva from the Altai Mountains?"

"Tuva is behind the next row of mountains to the east," I said.

"One of my dreams is to get to the Altai," said Dr. Keller, whose Ph.D. is in geology.

I was among friends.

Keller said, "I'll run this by our director. It shouldn't be any problem." We all shook hands.

As I left the Museum, I started talking to myself: "I can't believe it—it was so easy!" I began to sing a familiar melody but with different words. "Tannu Tuva, here we come!"

The Keller Accord

10 APPROVAL from the Natural History Museum's director, Dr. Craig Black, came quickly.

Meanwhile, Halley's comet was making its appearance in our corner of the solar system, so I went with Phoebe to South America to check it out. The Brazilian press called the faint comet with its diffuse tail "uma farça," and I agreed—the view had been much better from the local mountains and deserts near Los Angeles in February. But the night sky of the Southern Hemisphere was glorious, especially the Magellanic clouds (companion galaxies to our own, the Milky Way). Five weeks later, just after Ronald Reagan ordered Libya bombed in retaliation for a Syrian-backed attack on a bar in Berlin, we returned to Los Angeles amid extra-tight airline security.

There was no reply from the USSR Academy of Sciences to the Chief's letter, sent six weeks earlier. I discussed the matter with Glen, who offered the reassuring observation that it is quite normal for Soviets not to answer mail (!). I then called the Natural History Museum and suggested that Dr. Black also send letters to Alexandrov and Kapitsa, in case they thought Richard Feynman was not the right partner for them. I also acted on the plan suggested by Vainshtein in Sweden, and persuaded W. W. Norton to send a telex to VAAP proposing a popular book about Tuva.

At the end of April and in early May, a mysterious cloud caused Geiger counters all over Europe to crackle. Children in Poland were given doses of iodine. Reindeer were slaughtered in Lapland after eating moss soaked with radioactive rain. The world learned the name of a small Ukrainian village near the border of Byelorussia: Chernobyl. With such a crisis going on in the USSR, the chance of receiving a reply from the Academy of Sciences seemed remote indeed.

But the Natural History Museum had an ace in the hole: Sylvan Marshall, an illustrious Washington, D.C., lawyer who represented the Soviet Union in U.S. courts, had already discussed the Museum's interest in the exhibition with the USSR's acting ambassador. Marshall got his Soviet embassy friends to deliver Dr. Black's letter to the Academy of Sciences by diplomatic pouch.

Richard finished his work on the Rogers Commission in June. He looked tired and haggard. It turned out he had been under a lot of pressure to accept a "tenth recommendation," concocted after the commission had adjourned its last formal meeting. Feynman refused to be railroaded, and refrained from signing the report until the recommendation was removed. The Rogers Commission was praised from many quarters for its integrity and for setting a new standard for presidential commissions. Once again Richard managed to make Rogers look good even though he had gone against the Chairman's wishes. A real hero to the public now, Richard wanted to return to relative obscurity as quickly as possible and recuperate from the exhausting experience.

By mid-June there was still no reply from Moscow. So the next attempt at communication with the mysterious black hole was a telegram.

Again, silence.

In early July I received a telephone call from W. W. Norton: VAAP was in favor of the popular book on Tuva. VAAP requested that Norton send a sample contract; Norton got cold feet. Undaunted, I wrote to VAAP myself and asked whether they could arrange visas for the translator, the photographer, and me to visit Tuva.

I wrote Axel-Nilsson for advice. He suggested we communicate with the Soviets by telex, and sent Kapitsa's number. To our surprise the Natural History Museum did not have a telex machine, so the Chief sent a telex from Caltech asking whether Kapitsa had received our letters and telegram.

Miracle of miracles, an answer came back five days later:

THE QUESTION IS BEING DISCUSSED. OUR ANSWER
WILL COME IN NEXT TELEX.

Two weeks later my mother sent me an article from the *New Yorker* about the exhibition of French Impressionist paintings that was coming to the United States under the cultural agreement signed in Geneva by Reagan and Gorbachev. J. Carter Brown, director of the National Gallery of Art, described to a reporter how the exhibition had come about:

> It derives from a visit I paid in 1983 to Lugano, Switzerland, and to the Villa Favorita, a villa and museum maintained there by Baron Heinrich Thyssen-Bornemisza. We know the baron quite well. He is on our Trustees Council. He has a wonderful collection. . . . There hadn't been a chance of exchanging pictures back in 1980, for example, during the

boycott of the Olympics following the invasion of Afghani-
stan. But in 1983 everybody seemed to be for it. Secretary
Shultz; Arthur Hartman, our Ambassador to the Soviet
Union; Charles Wick, head of the United States Information
Agency—they were all for it. I thought we were set, and got
back here filled with hope.

Then, in September, we heard of the downing of the Korean airliner. Flight 007. I knew that our hopes had gone
down with that plane. But some instinct was at work in me,
and I proceeded as though we would have an exhibit after
all. . . . In matters of this kind, the political angle is both
possible and impossible, often at the same time. Politics in this
sort of agreement is really a roll of the dice. A man like Ar-
mand Hammer, for instance, never leaves the Soviet Union
without a signed agreement. Won't leave until he has a piece
of paper in his hand. [But] I went ahead and constructed the
galleries you were in this morning. I had a hunch something
would happen, and it paid off. First, though, there was a stag-
nant period. Everything was *nyet.* Not a chance. I said to
myself, We will have to wait for a cultural agreement. I had a
strange confidence that *one* thing would come out of a summit—a cultural agreement. That would be the meeting of the
minds. When the agreement finally came, in November of
1985, we were ready. We were all geared up. Cables went back
and forth. Curators went back and forth. The Soviets agreed
to send over forty pictures in eighty days. Quick movement
was required. We live, after all, in the real world, and one
never knows how long any of this harmony will last.

I could see that although our histories were similar (both
exhibitions had appeared in provincial museums in neutral
European countries), we amateurs were definitely at a disad-
vantage: the Friends of Tuva were trying to bring twenty
times more stuff from the USSR, but with only one high-level
Washington contact—the illustrious lawyer Sylvan Marshall.

By now a month had gone by with no further word from
Kapitsa.

Meanwhile, the Impressionist exhibition came to Los Angeles. I went over to appreciate all forty paintings of it, receiving an additional shot of cultural enrichment by renting a headset and listening to the recorded tour.

A few days after that, a delegation of Soviets from the Ministry of Culture came to town. Dr. Keller and Mrs. Black took the visitors to the holy shrine of Disneyland. Keller reported that during their excursion to the never-never land that Khrushchev never saw, the Soviets volunteered that our exhibition on the nomads of Eurasia was a more appropriate reflection of the cultures in the Soviet Union than was the collection of French Impressionist paintings currently on display in Los Angeles. The Ministry officials promised to check into its status when they returned to Moscow.

Before the delegation departed the United States, the telex operator at Caltech reported a message from Moscow addressed to Dr. Black:

FOR TALKS ON ORGANIZATION EXHIBITION "NOMADS OF EURASIA" IN UNITED STATES DESIRABLE MEETING IN MOSCOW AT END OF SEPTEMBER BEGINNING OCTOBER STOP ASK CONFIRM POSSIBILITY COMING TO MOSCOW MUSEUM REPRESENTATIVES ON THEIR EXPENSES AT MENTIONED TIME ON BUSINESS TOUR STOP

PROFESSOR KAPITSA USSR ACADEMY OF SCIENCES STOP

The USSR had accepted, at last! It had taken Keller five minutes to say yes to the exhibition; it had taken the Soviets five months.

Because Dr. Black was out of town, nothing was done about the telex for ten days. Then Nicholas Daniloff, a reporter for *U.S. News & World Report*, was detained in Moscow and put in the KGB's Lubyanka Prison on charges of spying. As J. Carter Brown said to the *New Yorker*, "one never knows how long any of this harmony will last."

Nevertheless, the Museum began making arrangements to have Dr. Keller and Sylvan Marshall visit Moscow at the beginning of October. (Dr. Black could not go then; he had another previously scheduled trip.) A few days later the United States allowed Gennadi Zakarov, a spy caught in New York, to leave the country. Daniloff, too, soon came home.

Richard and I prepared a background sheet on the major players in the USSR, Sweden, and Finland; we attached a copy of the protocol provided by Axel-Nilsson, and gave them to Dr. Keller for his negotiations.

One Saturday in September Phoebe and I received a telegram:

BOLSHOE SPASIBO ZA PRIGLASHENIE POLUCHIL POZDNO POZDRAVLIAIU S BRAKOSOCHETANIEM JELAIU SCHASTIA BLAGOPOLUCHIIA V SEMEINOI JIZNI JDU PISMA.
    DARYMA ONDAR

Glen Cowan was in Pasadena, so I asked him to translate it. The telegram said:

THANK YOU VERY MUCH FOR THE INVITATION. I RECEIVED IT LATE. I CONGRATULATE YOU ON YOUR WEDDING. I WISH YOU HAPPINESS AND WELL-BEING IN YOUR FAMILY LIFE. I AWAIT YOUR LETTERS.
    ONDAR DARYMA

Ondar's telegram was the last (and therefore the best-timed) greeting to arrive before Phoebe and I got married. In our wedding Richard was best man, while Alan, Glen, and my clown-diving friend Jeff Davis were the other groomsmen.

(For some reason I couldn't convince Phoebe to jump off a diving board with me to symbolize our plunge into married life.)

At the reception Richard, Glen, Phoebe, and I posed for a special picture: Glen held Ondar's telegram, while I held up a poster that said "Hello, Ondar Daryma California-from" in Tuvan.

The next day Phoebe and I departed for our honeymoon in the Ryukyu Islands, Hong Kong, and Korea. In Korea we rented a car and drove northeast, to Mt. Sorak National Park.

We reply to a telegram from our Tuvan pen pal Ondar Daryma. From left to right: Glen Cowan (holding telegram), Ralph Leighton (holding reply), Phoebe Kwan, Richard Feynman. (Courtesy Eugene Cowan.)

Blood-red maples matched the setting sun in the crisp fall air.

The following day we walked along a stream nestled in a gorge amid perfect scenery for an Oriental scroll painting. Stones were stacked at prominent points along the path. The German traveler Mänchen-Helfen had seen such cairns in Tuva in 1929!

I realized we were only one time zone away from Kyzyl: our pen pal Ondar Daryma was no doubt awake at that very moment, perhaps enjoying the same sunny weather on that glorious Sunday.

We came upon a temple wedged between a tall, thin mountain and the rushing stream below. The blissful Buddha inside was straight out of India, yet we were only a few miles from the Sea of Japan. Nearby, dozens of little white cloth strips decorated the bushes, just as I had seen in Armenia. Was this same custom independently invented, or—like Buddhism—was it carried on horseback five thousand miles across Asia by nomads and traders?

A little farther upstream we met some Korean families enjoying a picnic lunch. Two men sitting on their haunches, barbecuing strips of meat on a portable grill, motioned us to come over and join them. As the women and children looked on, one of the men poured some clear liquid into half an apple that had been hollowed out—an ingenious biodegradable cup (you eat it when you're finished)—and handed it to me. I thought of the bottled water we had bought in Seoul two days before, remembering that the name on the label resembled *sug*, the Tuvan word for water. I pointed to the liquid in my little apple cup and proudly said, "Su."

The host nodded his head and smiled, gesturing that I should drink it all in one shot.

As the fire poured down my throat and my face flushed crimson, the whole family laughed uproariously.

That afternoon we returned to Seoul on a nerve-racking, three-lane "expressway" that meandered through the mountains. Unwinding in our hotel room, we lounged on bedrolls spread out over the heated floor. Eventually I switched on the television set, just in time to catch the weather report on U.S. Armed Forces TV. From the satellite photo of East Asia I could tell that Tuva had indeed enjoyed fine weather that day.

Over the next few days Phoebe and I watched several events of the Asian Games in Seoul. Later, we went shopping in the tourist district of Itaewon. As we passed stands of counterfeit Louis Vuitton luggage and racks of pirated cassette tapes, Phoebe noticed a hat shop that specialized in custom designs. We commissioned two dozen black velvet baseball caps with "ТЫВА" and "TUVA" flanking the monument inspired by the eccentric Englishman, and had "Centre of Asia" written underneath it. I would hide the caps in my luggage and pass them out in Kyzyl when Richard, Glen, and I finally reached our goal together.

When we returned to Los Angeles, Ronald Reagan and Mikhail Gorbachev were preparing to meet in Reykjavik, Iceland. But I was more interested to know the fate of Dr. Keller in Moscow. Was our exhibition, with its many artifacts from Tuva, really coming to Los Angeles? And was a certain delegation from the Museum going to visit Kyzyl?

I called the Feynmans. Gweneth had no news about Dr. Keller, but told me that Richard had become ill the day after our wedding, and had checked into the hospital a week later—cancer had returned once again. Dr. Morton performed another daring operation, giving Richard yet another lease on life.

In my mail there were two letters from the USSR. One was from Moscow: VAAP could not arrange visas for us, so Vainshtein's plan of writing a popular book about Tuva hit a dead end.

The other letter was from Vladimir Lamin, the taciturn Siberian whom Glen and I had met in Sweden. He formally extended an invitation to Phoebe and me to visit him in Novosibirsk, from where he said he could arrange a trip to Tuva. Everything now depended on us—all we had to do was say yes. Lamin's letter concluded, "They say in Russia, 'Prepare sledge in summertime.' "

The next day, Phoebe and I went out to the UCLA Medical Center to visit Richard. Soon after we arrived, Dr. Keller and Jim Olson dropped in unexpectedly to give the Chief a personal report about Keller's trip to Moscow.

First of all, in Helsinki, Keller's hosts showed him an exhibition of Alaskan native artifacts collected by Arvid Adolf Etholén, a Finnish admiral, in the early nineteenth century—when Finland and Alaska were both part of the Russian Empire. "The Finns are only now preparing to show this collection for the first time," said Keller. "All these years it has been packed in the Museum's basement in Helsinki, undisturbed. The objects are in perfect condition."

Keller continued: "In contrast, the artifacts from Leningrad and Moscow which will be in the 'Crossroads' exhibition are in such bad shape that they will require major amounts of restoration work by the Smithsonian."

Then Keller reported that he met a Japanese delegation in Moscow that had been negotiating with the Soviets for two years—and still didn't have an agreement. "I got a little nervous when I heard that," he confessed. "But when Sylvan Marshall and I sat down with Kapitsa and Basilov, I said, 'Gentlemen, I think you know why we are all here. There are three guys from California who want to go to Tuva.' Everyone smiled. Then I pulled out the copy of the Swedish protocol you gave me, and they pulled out their copy of the same protocol—with a few changes. Marshall and I took the revised protocol to our hotel and looked it over. The next day we had an agreement, and here it is!" Dr. Keller handed the Chief a copy of the new protocol. "The exhibition will come to Los Angeles in January 1989."

"That's great!" said Richard. "What the others couldn't do in two years, you guys did in two days!"

"It's because *you* guys made all the preparations," said Keller.

The Chief turned to me, smiling broadly, and said, "You see, man? We're *professionals.* We're finders of international exhibitions!"

Dr. Keller continued, "While I was in Moscow, I discovered two more exhibitions we might bring to Los Angeles: a frozen baby mammoth—fur, flesh, and all—dug up in the permafrost of Siberia, and a collection of Fabergé carvings displayed at the Mineralogical Museum."[1]

As we were all congratulating each other, I couldn't help but ask a minor, technical question: "Is there a specific place in the protocol that says we'll get to Tuva?"

"Yes," said Keller. He showed me the last clause on the last page. It said, "The American side will attempt to find the means to send filmmakers for production of a documentary film on themes connected with the subject matter of the exhibition."

That was the plan hatched in Göteborg whereby Richard, Glen, and I—along with Christopher Sykes—would go to Tuva as museum representatives and make video recordings of archaeological sites.

"That's great!" I said. "We'll all go next summer. Tannu Tuva, here we come!"

The next day I replied to Lamin's invitation to visit Tuva via Novosibirsk. After reporting Keller's success with the Academy of Sciences, I said, "Now that the way is clear for the 'Three Musketeers' to visit Tuva together, you don't have to make any arrangements for Phoebe and me—unless you

---

[1]The Fabergé collection, as well as the Finnish admiral's collection of Alaskan native artifacts, came to the Natural History Museum in subsequent years.

want to consider your plan as a 'second sledge,' to be used if our 'first sledge' overturns."

I also Xeroxed the Chief's copy of the protocol and sent the English and Russian versions to Glen, who touched up the Soviets' translation. (It appears as Appendix A.)

A few days later, in Iceland, Mikhail Gorbachev proposed a mutual 50 percent reduction in all nuclear weapons if the United States would not deploy its "Star Wars" (SDI) in space. Ronald Reagan agreed to the dramatic proposal. It was a wise move: "Star Wars" was proving to be a fantasy; moreover, the vast majority of physicists in the country had refused to participate in this diversion from real science.[2] But then White House Chief of Staff Donald Regan stepped in and declared that President Reagan had not agreed to anything.

I imagined the following conversation between Secretary of State George Shultz and Soviet Foreign Minister Eduard Shevardnadze:

SHULTZ: "The world is disappointed that we have nothing to show as a result of this summit. Isn't there *some* agreement we can point to?"

SHEVARDNADZE: "Well, Mr. Secretary, I understand that our Academy of Sciences has just agreed to send a large museum exhibition to the United States. . . ."

Alas, there was no such conversation—at least no announcement of our exhibition. The next day, though, an

---

[2]A declaration of refusal to do any work associated with the SDI was one of the few petitions that Feynman ever signed. He also had the "Star Wars" project in mind when he wrote, "For a successful technology, reality must take precedence over public relations, for Nature cannot be fooled"—the concluding remark of his *Personal Observations on the Reliability of the Shuttle,* the subject of much wrangling with Chairman Rogers, which appears both in the official Commission report and in *What Do You Care What Other People Think?,* as Appendix F.

opinion piece by Kurt M. Campbell in the October 16th issue of the *Christian Science Monitor* had these words:

> In an era when the superpowers cannot seem to agree on anything—whether to suspend underground testing, what to do about "Star Wars," and ultimately, whether arms control is useful—the "Impressionists' Accord" [I read: the "Keller Accord"] serves as a refreshing exception to the general lack of progress in bilateral relations. . . .
>
> While some would dismiss these modest steps as irrelevant in comparison with the life-or-death questions of the strategic dialogue, the fact remains that the exchange of Impressionist paintings is one of the few rays of hope in an otherwise dead-locked agenda of exotic weaponry, verification disputes, and underground nuclear testing. In this new phase of Soviet-American relations, perhaps it's time for the arms controllers to look to the artists for ideas and inspiration.

I didn't mind that artifacts from the nomads of Eurasia were not as famous as French Impressionist paintings; the uplifting words from the *Christian Science Monitor* made me feel like the wild scheme cooked up in Vainshtein's apartment could do more than simply get us to Tuva—it might even help bring peace to the world!

I quickly returned to more practical matters: now that the "Keller Accord" would bring the Nomads exhibition to the United States, what was our next step in reaching Tuva? Become staff members of the Natural History Museum, of course. But that would have to wait until Richard recovered from his surgery.

To build up his stamina after he got out of the hospital, the Chief and I took daily walks from his home, which we imagined to be Kyzyl. After a few days we got to Shagonar, down the Yenisei River from Kyzyl, at Braeburn Avenue. A week later we made it to Chadan, once home of Tuva's largest lamasery, over at Porter Street. After a few weeks we made it all the way to Teeli, at the end of the Khemchik Valley, down at Allen Avenue.

To further prepare ourselves for our journey, I copied out words from the Tuvan-Mongolian-Russian phrasebook onto little yellow flash cards. As we walked the streets of Altadena, Richard and I chanted, "Ujurashkanyvyska öörüp tur men,"[3] and the like.

Another way to build up the Chief's strength was through drumming. We imagined finding an old shaman's drum inside a yurt and bringing it to life. An alternate fantasy was performing rhythms from the hit San Francisco ballet *Cycles of Superstition* in Kyzyl's drama theater.

When Richard was strong enough to visit the Museum, we went down and got our official photo-ID badges. The next time Glen came to Pasadena he went to the Museum and got a badge as well. Upon his return to Berkeley he immediately noticed its effect on his social life: telling people that he was a research associate at the Natural History Museum of Los Angeles County got him farther than saying he was a graduate student in physics.

Now that we were members of its staff, the Museum sent a telex to Andrei Kapitsa declaring its intention to send a filmmaker and its newly appointed research associates to archaeological sites, as specified under Article 10 of the protocol. Our plan for getting to Tuva was right on track.

But this time, Kapitsa did not reply promptly to our telex—there was no reply at all.

I sent a telegram to Sevyan Vainshtein informing him of our telex to Kapitsa. I also prepared a detailed letter for Basilov outlining our proposed trip. Although I had wanted to say that time was of the essence (since the Chief wasn't going to be able to fend off cancer forever), Richard told me not to say

[3]"Meeting-mutual-having-our-at happy am I," or "Pleased to meet you."

anything about his health—he didn't want to scare the Soviets. Instead, he advised me to explain that although the Academy of Sciences might think a Nobel prize–winning physicist would expect to sleep in a hotel or a hunting lodge, "Professor Feynman prefers sleeping outside, under the stars." And to make the Soviets' job of arranging our trip easier, we would bring our own tents and sleeping bags. All we needed were a few vehicles and a minimum of escorts.

I made Xeroxes of my USSR road atlas and my Defense Mapping Agency chart of Tuva, and highlighted several possible routes. One followed the main road from Novosibirsk through Biysk and Gorno-Altaisk (site of the famous Pazaryk burial mounds) into Mongolia. We would leave the main road before Ulaangom, enter Tuva at Khandagaity, and pass through Chadan before reaching Kyzyl. The other routes, over smaller roads, stayed within the USSR.

Before sending the package of materials to Basilov, I sent them to Keller and Olson. Olson replied with a letter:

Dear Ralph:

Please hold off on sending your letter to Dr. Basilov. Your enthusiasm for getting to Tuva is very infectious, but you need to slow down. . . .

We recognize that without you and Dr. Feynman we would not be in possession of the protocol for the exhibition "Nomads of Eurasia." We feel, however, we have a lot at stake in terms of establishing our credibility for this and future exchanges. We all need to be in agreement on how we should proceed. In light of this, I feel it is important for you to send me copies of any correspondence concerning this project for approval before it is sent out. . . .

Not wanting my work to go to waste, I sent the package of materials to Vladimir Lamin in Novosibirsk for his comments. He wrote back later: "To tell the truth, some points of that list can irresistibly provoke an ironical smile. By its speed and difficulty, your itinerary is easily comparable with the international auto rally Paris-Dakar. . . ."

Christmas was approaching, and the hottest gift item that year was a game called Trivial Pursuit. I made a special edition of the game, called Tuva Trivia, and sent it out as a greeting card. Photographer Yasushi Ohnuki's wife, Masako, provided the best trivia question of all: "From what country is the actor Maxim Munzuk, who starred in the Akira Kurosawa film *Dersu Uzala?*"[4]

My one-track mind was vindicated: the actor who played

---

[4]For those trivia buffs who are curious, here's how the game went:

Congratulations! You are the proud owner of America's ultimate trivia game, the one for intrepid trivia buffs who want to impress their few remaining friends by successfully answering questions about the world's most obscure trivia topic: TUVA!

TUVA TRIVIA doesn't waste your time by making you throw dice and move little plastic pieces around a silly board; TUVA TRIVIA does not leave it to chance to help determine whether you score the greatest trivia triumph known to man; TUVA TRIVIA gets right to the point by making you answer incredibly difficult, do-or-die questions from six different categories. Are you ready to take the challenge?

1. GEOGRAPHY: What country has a monument on the banks of the Yenisei River marking the (incorrectly determined) center of Asia?
2. HISTORY: What country was nominally independent from 1921 to 1944, was visited by Otto Mänchen-Helfen in 1929, and issued triangular and diamond-shaped postage stamps in 1936?
3. SCIENCE & NATURE: In what country are camels, reindeer, yaks, cattle, sheep, and goats all herded within 150 miles of its capital city, Kyzyl?
4. SPORTS: In what country is basketball called *sags bömbög?*
5. LITERATURE: From what country is the compiler of Soyot folk literature Ondar Daryma?
6. ENTERTAINMENT: From what country is the actor Maxim Munzuk, who starred in the Akira Kurosawa film *Dersu Uzala?*

If you get through all the cards in one turn, you have achieved a feat worthy of qualifying you to become an honorary member of Friends of Tuva! On the other hand, if you make so much as even *one* mistake, you not only lose the game, you also must face the ego-shattering fact that you are not as trendy as you thought you were!

the role of Dersu really *was* a Tuvan! I decided to write a fan letter to Tuva's internationally acclaimed movie star—in Tuvan, of course. Thumbing through the Tuvan-Mongolian-Russian phrasebook, I was able to piece together sentences like "I film *Dersu Uzala* California-in saw I" and "Summer-in Tuva-to come-will I: meeting-mutual possible?" And to fatten up my letter I found a particularly flowery phrase: "From the depths of my soul I greet you, wish you success in your work, good health, and happiness in your life."

Nearly six weeks after we had telexed Kapitsa, I received a message from our "back channel"—in the parlance of the unfolding Iran-Contra scandal. It said:

PLEASE REPEAT YOUR TELEX TO A P KAPITSA ABOUT ANTICIPATED FILM PLANNING TRIP TO CENTRAL ASIAN ARCHAEOLOGICAL SITES IN SUMMER 1987 REGARDS

VAINSHTEIN

We dutifully repeated the telex.

The next day, we heard some good news from the USSR: Andrei Sakharov was released from exile in Gorky and allowed to return to Moscow. Within days he appeared live on "This Week with David Brinkley." Mikhail Gorbachev was beginning to make his mark on Soviet society and on world history.

The Trip Is Arranged

A NATIVE of Pasadena, I watched the 1987 Tournament of Roses Parade on television— from San Francisco, where Phoebe and I were visiting two of her sisters. At the end of the parade came an equestrian group from Winnemucca, Nevada, riding small horses called Bashkir Curlies. The name rang a bell: *premier danseur* Rudolf Nureyev came from Ufa, capital of the Bashkir ASSR.[1] Nureyev was a Tatar. Were Bashkir Curlies related somehow to the hearty horses that carried the Tatars across the Eurasian steppe?

I had a vision. It was January 1, 1989, and I was once again watching the Rose Parade on

11

---

[1]Whereas Tuva was the last Autonomous Soviet Socialist Republic (ASSR) to join the Soviet Union (in 1944), the Bashkir ASSR—located just west of the Ural Mountains—was the first (in 1919). The native Bashkir people, Muslim by faith, are a mixture of Turkic and Mongolian (that is, Tatar) and Finno-Ugric tribes; thus they are distantly related to the Tuvans.

television. The announcer says, "And now, ladies and gentlemen, we have an equestrian group from the Soviet Union:
they are from Kyzyl, Tuva (known to stamp collectors as
Tannu Tuva), a land tucked away between Siberia and Mongolia. Our horsemen, descendants of Genghis Khan's armies,
are riding Bashkir Curlies, kindly lent by the Bashkir Curly
Registry of Winnemucca, Nevada. They are on their way to
the Natural History Museum of Los Angeles County, where
the exhibition 'Nomads of Eurasia' is opening later this
month."

What a promo!

Shortly after I returned to Los Angeles a reply came from
Kapitsa. The date was January 16, only two months after we
had sent him the telex declaring our intention to send a
filmmaker and research associates to archaeological sites.

WE INFORM IN ORDER TO MAKE VIDEO AND DOCU-
MENTARY FILMS FOR BROADCAST ON NOMADS OF
EURASIA YOU SHOULD APPLY TO ALEXANDER
SURIKOV, CHAIRMAN OF SOVINFILM DEPART-
MENT OF THE STATE COMMITTEE ON CINEMATOG-
RAPHY. THE OFFICIAL ADDRESS IS SKATERNII
PEREULOK 20, MOSCOW.

We prepared a friendly letter to Mr. Surikov and sent it
five days later. To save time and avoid confusion, we put
Surikov in direct contact with Basilov to work out the details,
and sent a copy to Kapitsa. I also informed Vainshtein of
these developments.

While we were waiting for a reply from Sovinfilm, a letter
came from Kyzyl—from Maxim Munzuk! Immediately Richard and I dusted off our dictionaries, phrasebook, and *Tuvan
Manual.* The first line amounted to Munzuk being glad I had
seen *Dersu Uzala;* the next line said it was interesting that I

wrote in Tuvan. Then came a long string of words we couldn't make head nor tail of—something about "work-goal," "life-condition," and "mouth-gift." Then came some simpler phrases again: "Where-from?" and "What work do you?" Finally came the Tuvan words for "One-not Tuva-to come-you-will, meeting-mutual will we."

I was crushed. It appeared that I wouldn't be able to meet Tuva's internationally acclaimed movie star.

"What makes you so sure that 'one-not' means Munzuk can't meet you?" said Richard.

" 'Bir' is most certainly 'one,' and 'eves,' is undoubtedly 'not,' " I replied.

"What about 'one-not' as a combination?" asked the Chief, who always believed in rechecking the data before proposing a theory.

"There are dozens of combinations with 'one,' " I said, "but— Hey, look! Here's 'bir eves'—I didn't see it before. The combination means 'esli' in Russian." I reached for my pocket Russian-English dictionary. " 'Esli' comes out 'if.' So the sentence reads 'If Tuva-to come-you-will, meeting-mutual will we.' "

I could meet Tuva's movie star after all—if we got to Kyzyl, that is. Relieved, we turned to the lengthy phrase that we couldn't decipher before.

While rechecking various words in combination, it suddenly hit me: Munzuk was repeating the same flowery phrase I had used to fatten up my letter to him—followed by the question "Where-from?"

I laughed. "I can imagine how my letter looked to him," I said. "First comes all this fractured Tuvan: 'Me *Dersu Uzala* California seen. Much good-good.' Then out of the blue comes this eloquent stuff: 'From the depths of my soul I greet you, wish you success in your work, good health, and happiness in your life.' No wonder he asked 'Where-from': it stuck out like a sore thumb!" I realized that our "Tuvan" was equally confusing (and perhaps just as funny) to Ondar Daryma.

As February flew by, we heard nothing from Sovinfilm. We sent a telex to Surikov asking whether he had received our January letter.

No reply.

Then I saw a report on the MacNeil/Lehrer Newshour that featured three Soviet women. One of them worked as a translator for Sovinfilm! I quickly wrote down her name—Yelena Zagrevskaya—and wrote her: might she have seen our letter to Surikov?

Ms. Zagrevskaya replied promptly. Although she no longer worked at Sovinfilm (she just stopped in to pick up my letter), she found out that our letter had indeed arrived, and that Sovinfilm had contacted Basilov's office—but he was out of town until the end of March.

To pass the time I decided to order a new Landsat photo of Tuva to replace the one I had given Sevyan Vainshtein. This time I would order two of them (taken at slightly different angles), and try for a 3-D effect. As before, I asked for the latest printout of everything from 49° to 54° North and from 88° to 99° East.

When I received the printout, I made an informal survey by tallying how many Landsat photographs with less than 30 percent less cloud cover were taken over Tuva each month during the past ten years. June and July were by far the clearest months (95 and 94 photos, respectively), while May came next (70 photos). November and February were the cloudiest (15 each). We would try to go to Tuva in June.[2]

There was also some curious news in the cover letter:

[2]A June or July day is not necessarily six times more likely to be sunny than one in November or February: because daylight is twice as long in summer as in winter, there is twice the chance of getting a photograph regardless of the cloud cover.

Dear EOSAT customer,

As you may know, beginning July 1, 1986, EOSAT made a decision to suspend the special data acquisition charge through the end of 1986. The response from our customers was very positive, and consequently, EOSAT has decided to continue the acquisition free period through calendar year 1987. . . . If you wish to ensure that the scene has less than 30% cloud cover, there is still a $275 charge.

I telephoned EOSAT. "Let me see if I've got it straight," I said. "If I want you to point a satellite at a specific place on the globe—just for me—you guys will do it free of charge . . ."

"That's right," the service rep replied, "providing you buy the photograph at the regular price, of course."

"Of course. How quickly do you take the photograph?"

"Within twenty-four hours," the rep said. "We have governments and companies asking for fresh information all the time—things like forest fires and oil spills can be seen on Landsat photos. What particular place are you interested in?"

I picked out a spot in Tuva and read out the coordinates.

"Oh, I'm sorry, sir. That part of the world cannot be accessed because the relay satellite needed to transmit the instructions to Landsat blew up with the shuttle. We were going to put it into geosynchronous orbit over the Indian Ocean."

Until then I had thought the only connection between *Challenger* and Tuva was Richard Feynman. At any rate, I went ahead and ordered an existing pair of photos, and was able to achieve a fairly good 3-D effect of the Sayan Mountains.

In early March I telephoned Christopher Sykes in London to report the latest lack of progress. Chris said he had just talked to a carpet collector who had traveled to closed areas of the Soviet Union before, and gave me the man's number.

The carpet collector offered the following advice: taking cameras or video equipment into a closed area of the USSR is next to impossible—it's hard enough just to get yourself there. He also counseled, "Stay with one circle of friends." I didn't know what to do with that advice.

A few days later I received a telegram in German from our back channel: "SOVINFILM IST EINVERSTANDEN"— Sovinfilm agrees!

A few days later the Museum received a letter from Basilov, apparently written shortly before he left Moscow:

> Prof. A. P. Kapitsa has given me his copy of your letter of January 21, 1987, addressed to Alexander Surikov of Sovinfilm. . . . May I suggest you send them as soon as possible a new letter on the same subject with the following exact information:
> 1) how many persons are you going to send to the USSR;
> 2) their names, positions, etc.;
> 3) the places you are planning to visit;
> 4) how long the group will stay in the USSR;
> 5) whether you will bring your own cameras and cassettes;
> 6) what kind of help or collaboration can be made by Sovinfilm. It is probably better to request their help; otherwise they will have no reason to supervise or participate in your work of making video recordings.

Then Basilov suggested nine places to visit, with Tuva buried in the middle. He continued:

> If you get permission to carry out your program (or at least part of it), your group will be definitely provided with the guidance of Academy of Sciences specialists.

Keller, Olson, Feynman, and I discussed what to do next. I recalled Basilov's advice, given to Glen and me in Sweden, that Sykes must not come to Tuva as a representative of the BBC: "Otherwise, Soviet TV will become involved, and they will send representatives with you everywhere you go." Now, from Moscow, Basilov was playing a different tune: "It is probably better to request Sovinfilm's help; otherwise they will have no reason to supervise or participate in your work of making video recordings." We had no reason to think that Sovinfilm was any different from Soviet TV, so how could we reconcile Basilov's contradictory suggestions?

"Those suggestions are not necessarily contradictory," observed the Chief. "If we accept that Mr. Basilov can't write freely from Moscow, he might have to phrase his advice carefully: if we request Sovinfilm's help, they will have to supervise our work—and we don't want that."

Then I recalled the advice of the carpet collector: "Stay with one circle of friends." It began to make sense now.

"In other words, don't change horses in the middle of the stream," said Keller. Kapitsa had bucked us off the Academy horse; we had no "friends" at Sovinfilm.

We formulated a strategy: politely keep Sovinfilm at arm's length, dangling the possibility of a full-blown filming trip in 1988 (which means money for Sovinfilm); meanwhile, try to stay on the Academy horse, with our original "circle of friends." We sent letters by express mail to Sovinfilm, Kapitsa, and Basilov, emphasizing that our 1987 trip was mainly for purposes related to the exhibition; therefore we would prefer that it be arranged by the Academy of Sciences.

Keller's allusion to horses revived my Rose Parade vision. I contacted the Tournament of Roses Association and got the address of the Bashkir Curly Registry in Winnemucca, Nevada. I also found out how much it would cost to enter an equestrian group in the parade: due to liability insurance premiums, the fees had gone up—to $35 per rider.

Now *there's* something we can afford, I thought to myself. National exposure on TV for only $35 per rider is a bargain! The deadline for the 1989 parade was in May 1988, so I had a little more than a year to put the project together. I could make preliminary arrangements during our upcoming trip to Tuva: all I needed to do was get a color photo of some Tuvan horsemen in costume. Despite my enthusiasm, I decided not to tell Keller and Olson about this plan until it became more fully developed. Then they could decide whether the Museum wanted publicity in the Rose Parade or not.

At the end of March I received a letter from Lamin:

> Please be informed about final decisive plan of your stay in Novosibirsk and Tuva. . . .
>
> Our arrival on July 10, but not later than July 15, is already agreed and coordinated by the Director of the Tuvinian Institute, Dr. Y. Aranchyn. . . . We'll stay about 10 days. . . . This time, by opinion of our Tuvinian colleagues, would be quite sufficient to:
>
> 1) see all sights of Tuvinian capital Kyzyl;
> 2) visit Tuvinian Institute of Language, Literature, and History and meet the collaborators;
> 3) have a trip to Arzhan [excavation site of the large, bronze plaque from Scythian times depicting a coiled panther (featured in Vainshtein's book on Tuvan art and prominent in the Nomads exhibition)];
> 4) visit kumiss farm;
> 5) have a journey to some interesting places in Tuva;
> 6) satisfy your other interests concerned with exploration of Tuva and its history.
>
> . . . Now about going through necessary formalities for visa. Dear Ralph, you ought to apply to Soviet embassy or to Soviet consulate and take special visa form for guests, fulfill it, and officially register it. Then you are to send this registered visa form as soon as possible to me. . . . After receiving it, I'll send your invitation privately or through Ministry of Foreign Affairs of the USSR.

This is the last stage of going through necessary formalities and making official fulfillment.

From my side all other formalities and agreements are already done.

Looking forward to meeting with you again soon,

Vladimir Lamin

Lamin's "second sledge" was ready to go. It was now up to Phoebe and me to accept the ride or not.

Between sets of drumming I discussed Lamin's invitation with the Chief.

"Right now we're having trouble getting Sovinfilm and the Academy of Sciences to even acknowledge our telexes," he said. "In contrast, Mr. Lamin, in Novosibirsk, is doing things on his own initiative, trying to help us as best he can."

I recalled that the only Americans to reach Tuva—Owen Lattimore and, later, the three botanists—had their trips arranged in Novosibirsk. "The only problem is, Lamin can only invite one of us," I lamented.

"Suppose, for a moment, that Novosibirsk *is* the only way to get to Tuva," replied Richard. "If that's the case, you and Phoebe should go there first with Lamin and set up everything so we can all go together later."

"That won't be the way we planned it," I said. "But if that's the only way for all of us to go, I'll do it. It won't hurt to send in my visa application in any case."

The next day I sent away for the special visa forms as Lamin had instructed. At the same time, I requested regular visa application forms for all of us: I had read that things are usually done in a big rush at the last minute in the USSR; experienced travelers reported that Soviet visas often reach you the day before your departure, so it's a good idea to have your applications filled out well in advance.

Since our dream of entering Tuva from the south was not yet completely dead, I also wrote to the Mongolian embassy in London.[3] That way we could take our completed visa applications to the Mongolian embassy in Moscow for processing on the spot.

At the end of April Christopher Sykes reluctantly took his name off the list of Tuva trip participants, because he had to make commitments for the summer. He arranged for an excellent replacement: André Singer, a dashing young fellow Briton, was a visiting professor at USC, right across the street from the Natural History Museum. Singer brought impressive credentials: an anthropologist by training, he had filmed nomads in Sinkiang[4] and in Afghanistan's Wakhan corridor, the gash in the Hindu Kush that separated the Russian and British empires. He had been to the Soviet Union several times and had met Basilov.

Keller invited Singer to meet us at the Museum. Dr. Singer's first question was: after covering the Scythians, the Huns, and the ancient Turks, why did the exhibition not include a section on the Mongols, the greatest of the "imperial nomads," whose influence is still felt today in the structure of the Soviet state? Keller, Olson, Feynman, and I realized how ignorant we were about the subject at hand, and agreed that Singer should be Basilov's counterpart. He was immediately named director of the Nomads exhibition.

As for our plans to make video recordings of archaeological sites, Singer suggested that he first film Owen Lattimore, the world's foremost authority on Inner Asian nomads, whom he knew personally. Then the rest of us, assisted by one of his graduate students in anthropology, would go to Tuva

---

[3]Although diplomatic relations had just been established between the United States and Mongolia in January of that year (1987), there was as yet no Mongolian embassy in Washington. The United States, in deference to China (and later, Taiwan), had refused to recognize Mongolian independence for sixty-five years.

[4]His documentary film *Kazakhs: Horsemen of China* had just aired on PBS.

and look for contemporary examples of nomadism as described by Lattimore. If we brought back good material on videotape, Singer could use it to raise the necessary funds for a full documentary film in 1988.[5]

A few days later Singer got in touch with Basilov by telephone. Although it meant much more work, Basilov agreed to expand the exhibition to include the Mongols—perhaps in honor of Owen Lattimore's participation in the project. There would now be more than one thousand artifacts, the largest collection ever to travel from the USSR to the USA!

As May approached, we became increasingly nervous about our trip. We still had heard nothing officially from Sovinfilm or from the Academy of Sciences. Nevertheless, I made flight reservations for three different dates from Los Angeles to Moscow on three different airlines. Then I turned on the TV for hours at a time, day after day: Richard Secord was providing the best entertainment on television since Watergate. But when Secord's testimony was over, I couldn't ignore Moscow's silence any longer. Two months had passed since we had informed Sovinfilm and the Academy of Sciences that we wanted the latter to arrange our trip. With the Museum's approval I telephoned Basilov myself and told him of our consternation.

"I understand, Ralph," replied Basilov in his characteristically smooth way. "Recently I got the letter from your museum with this information. It is very wise that you do *not* contact officially the Academy of Sciences, because it is better for you to make the official contact with Sovinfilm."

Our strategy of staying with the same "circle of friends" wasn't working. The Academy of Sciences, for whatever reason, just wouldn't have us. We were stuck with Sovinfilm.

[5]Singer cautioned us that officially, nomadism no longer existed in the Soviet Union—but he was confident we would run into plenty of examples in Tuva. However, so as not to embarrass our hosts, we would continue to say our objective was archaeological sites.

Then I expressed our concern that time was running out.

"I understand, Ralph. I recently came home from England. I will include myself in the negotiations with Sovinfilm and will try to accelerate the process. But really, I am nobody to them. They have only one partner, and that is you, the American side. I can only give them some hints and advice." Basilov suggested focusing our efforts on fewer regions.

Keller sent another telex to Sovinfilm:

DEAR MR. SURIKOV,

PLEASE INFORM US OF THE STATUS OF OUR PRO-POSAL, AND OUR COSTS, FOR 28 JUNE 1987 PLAN-NING TRIP. REFER TO 21 JANUARY AND 24 MARCH LETTERS. MOST INTERESTED IN KAZAKH-KIRGHIZ, ALTAI-TUVA PARTS. WE EMPHASIZE THIS TRIP IS ONLY TO PRODUCE PRELIMINARY VIDEO MATERI-ALS, NOT TO MAKE ACTUAL DOCUMENTARY FILM. THIS TRIP IS NECESSARY TO OBTAIN FUNDING FOR FULL DOCUMENTARY, TO BE FILMED WITH YOU IN 1988. PLEASE TELEX C/O FEYNMAN, 188192 CAL-TECH PSD.

Four days later, a telex came to Caltech:

DEAR DR KELLER:

WE WOULD LIKE TO INFORM YOU THAT YOUR PRO-JECT, NOMADS OF EURASIA, IS BEING PREPARED NOW BY SOVINFILM, TOGETHER WITH THE USSR ACADEMY OF SCIENCES. SOVINFILM IS THE ONLY ORGANIZATION DEALING WITH RENDERING FACILITIES TO FOREIGN COMPANIES FOR SHOOT-ING IN THE USSR.

BEST REGARDS,

ALEXANDER SURIKOV, PRESIDENT

Acknowledgment at last!

I began studying my little yellow flash cards with intensity—the Tuvan phrases on them became mantras which I chanted over and over while stuck in traffic. On the open road I accompanied the powerful drone of my car's diesel motor with weak renditions of throat singing.

At the end of May a nineteen-year-old German pulled off a stunt that made sneaking into Tuva dressed as shepherds look simple: on Border Guards' Day, Matthias Rust flew a Cessna from Finland to Moscow, buzzed the Kremlin a few times, and landed on Red Square. Although he may have succeeded in his "mission of peace" by giving Gorbachev a pretext to fire the old-guard defense minister, Rust had to spend some time in jail for his feat.

Throughout the first two weeks of June—now it was Elliott Abrams, Albert Hakim, and Fawn Hall testifying about Iran-Contra—I was on the phone every other day with Basilov. By this time our telephone and telex bills could have paid for a round-trip ticket to Moscow, leading us to wonder whether one of us should have flown ahead and conducted the negotiations in person. At any rate, Basilov reported that the Altai and Kazakhstan had yet to give their permission, but Tuva and Kirghizia said yes.

"Great!" I replied, my heart pounding. "Our visa applications are ready! I'll send them by express mail to the Soviet embassy today!"

The Museum immediately telexed Sovinfilm and requested official confirmation of our trip by June 17.

June 17 came and went with no response from Sovinfilm.

More phone calls to Basilov, but still no confirmation from Sovinfilm. What was causing the delay? Already I had been forced to cancel two of the three sets of flight reservations I had made.

Thomas Luehrsen, the graduate student in anthropology brought in by André Singer, had been to the USSR before—

as well as to Indonesia and China. He blurted out, "Why don't you just ask point-blank how much money Sovinfilm wants to confirm our trip?"

It sounded crude, but we were desperate.

The next day, Basilov reported that it would cost 50,000 rubles—more than $80,000—for Sovinfilm to arrange our six-week trip!

"They must think we're a bunch of big-time Hollywood producers!" I said. We discussed what we could afford for the entire trip and settled on a limit of 14,000 rubles. With Keller we quickly formulated a telex and sent it to Sovinfilm:

DEAR MR SURIKOV,

I AM DELIGHTED TO HEAR THAT SOVINFILM WILL ARRANGE THE FILM PLANNING TRIP. WE ARE ABLE TO PAY 14,000 RUBLES TO COVER ALL EXPENSES (EXCEPT FOOD) FOR 30 DAYS FOR 7 PARTICIPANTS.

OUR ONLY AVAILABLE CONNECTING FLIGHT AR-RIVES MOSCOW JULY 5. TO RECEIVE VISAS IN TIME, SEND OFFICIAL INVITATION TO ME IMMEDIATELY BY TELEX OR TELEGRAM CONFIRMING THE TRIP WITH THE NAMES OF PARTICIPANTS: GLEN COWAN, RICHARD AND GWENETH FEYNMAN, PHOEBE KWAN, RALPH LEIGHTON, THOMAS LUEHRSEN, AND JAMES OLSON. (MR. SYKES IS UN-ABLE TO PARTICIPATE.)

BEST REGARDS,

PETER KELLER C/O RICHARD FEYNMAN 188192 CAL-TECH   PSD

No reply.

I called Basilov again. He said our trip was being handled by a woman named Marina, and gave me her telephone num-ber at Sovinfilm. The deadline for canceling our last reservation from Los Angeles to Moscow was only one day away. In desperation, we sent the following telex:

ATTENTION! URGENT MESSAGE: UNLESS WE RE-CEIVE YOUR OFFICIAL INVITATION TODAY, WE WILL LOSE OUR FLIGHT RESERVATIONS.

That night, I telephoned Sovinfilm, and talked with Marina. The Chief advised me to be friendly (friendliness is disarming, he said), even though we were mad as hell at Sovinfilm's treatment of us. I asked Marina about the status of our trip.

"We are in this moment arranging everything," she said.

"Could you tell me, please, how much the trip will cost us?"

"I do not know, exactly," replied Marina. "Perhaps 28,000 or 29,000 rubles—maybe more." She sounded like a Mafiosa dictating the price of protection for a pizza parlor.

"We have only 14,000 rubles to spend," I protested plaintively. "Why does it cost so much?"

"You will need extra tickets. You will need extra luggage . . ." The specter of Marina and a gang of Sovinfilm thugs following us around—at our expense, no less—enraged me. Nevertheless, I tried to be amiable.

Marina must have taken me for a fool.

The next morning, the Chief called me up.

"Hey, man, a telex from Sovinfilm came in this morning . . ."

"Oh yeah?"

"Yeah. I'll read it to you:

"DEAR DR KELLER,

"THIS IS TO CONFIRM THAT GLEN COWAN, RICH-ARD AND GWENETH FEYNMAN, PHOEBE KWAN, RALPH LEIGHTON, THOMAS LUEHRSEN, AND

JAMES OLSON ARE INVITED TO PARTICIPATE IN
FILM PLANNING TRIP IN USSR FROM 5 JULY TO 10
AUGUST. IN THIS CONNECTION, PLEASE DEPOSIT
THE EQUIVALENT OF 14,000 RUBLES AT CURRENT
RAXEEE RATES INTO ACCOUNT #179562 OF THE
BANK FOR FOREIGN ECONOMIC AFFAIRS."

"That's weird, Chief," I said. "I talked to Marina last
night, and she said the trip would cost us more than double
that amount."

"When did you talk to her?"

"At midnight, our time—11 A.M. in Moscow."

"Well, this telex was sent at 4:45 P.M. in Moscow, and was
signed by Surikov. I think he overruled Marina. I think we're
in!"

"I hope so, Chief."

"Let's call Keller at the Museum and see what he says."

Keller advised us to contact Sylvan Marshall, the Washington, D.C., lawyer who had helped him negotiate the protocol
with the Soviets. I read the telex to Mr. Marshall, and asked
first about the "RAXEEE" rates mentioned in the telex.

"There's the official rate, of course—about $1.65 a ruble.
But I've never heard of RAXEEE rates."

Then I told Marshall about the inconsistency between my
conversation with Marina and the telex from Surikov.

Marshall recommended we send the following telex immediately:

DEAR MR SURIKOV,

THANK YOU FOR SENDING INVITATION FOR JULY 5
TO AUGUST 10. WE ARE READY TO TRANSFER THE
US DOLLAR EQUIVALENT OF 14,000 RUBLES. PLEASE
CONFIRM BY TELEX TODAY THAT THIS SUM IS ALL
WE HAVE TO PAY FOR TOTAL EXPENSES (EXCEPT
FOOD) FOR ENTIRE TRIP IN THE USSR. ADDITIONAL

FUNDS ARE NOT AVAILABLE. ALSO, CONFIRM
WHICH REGIONS WE WILL BE VISITING. IMMEDIATE
RESPONSE ESSENTIAL.

BEST REGARDS,

PETER KELLER C/O RICHARD FEYNMAN 188192 CAL-
TECH PSD

While we were waiting for Sovinfilm's reply, the Chief
figured out what RAXEEE rates were: "There's apparently no
way to erase anything on a telex machine, so you just write
EEE after the mistake. So RAXEEE was just a mistake."

As I humored the airline into keeping our reservations an
extra day, we waited anxiously for Sovinfilm's reply. The next
morning I called the telex operator at Caltech. Yes, there was
a telex for us:

IN CONNECTION WITH YOUR FILM PLANNING TRIP,
YOU MAY DEPOSIT THE EQUIVALENT OF 10,000 RU-
BLES INTO ACCOUNT #179562 OF THE BANK FOR
FOREIGN ECONOMIC AFFAIRS. THE REST WILL BE
NEGOTIATED UPON YOUR ARRIVAL IN MOSCOW
ON 5 JULY.

Now we were *sure* that Sovinfilm was a gang of Russian
Mafiosi!

"Piss on them!" the Chief sneered. "I'll have nothing more
to do with Sovinfilm!" I suggested we telex Surikov with a
three-word message: GO TO HELL. But André Singer, who
had just returned from filming Owen Lattimore, advised us
that according to Central Asian bazaar etiquette, we must not
be the ones to break off negotiations: we must force the other
party to do it. The Chief immediately agreed with the idea.
Furthermore, Sovinfilm was still our best chance of getting to
Tuva together—we couldn't give up now! We sent the following telex:

DEAR MR SURIKOV,

UNFORTUNATELY, 14,000 RUBLES IS ALL WE HAVE
BEEN ABLE TO RAISE. OF COURSE WE CANNOT
COME TO MOSCOW KNOWING THAT OUR COSTS
COULD EXCEED OUR FUNDS, SO WE HAD TO CAN-
CEL OUR FLIGHT RESERVATIONS FOR JULY 5. WE
WOULD APPRECIATE IT VERY MUCH IF YOU
WOULD CONFIRM WHETHER THE TRIP MUST NOW
BE CANCELLED OR WHETHER A MORE LIMITED
ITINERARY IS STILL POSSIBLE FOR 14,000 RUBLES.

WHATEVER THE OUTCOME, WE THANK YOU ALL,
ESPECIALLY MARINA, TO WHOM RALPH SPOKE ON
THE PHONE, FOR YOUR EFFORTS IN TRYING TO
HELP US.

BEST REGARDS,

PETER KELLER C/O RICHARD FEYNMAN 188192 CAL-
TECH PSD

A week passed with no reply. The horse we were told to
lasso and ride to Tuva had galloped away to greener pastures.

Catalina Cowboys

Shortly after July 4 I heard a report on National Public Radio about the Moscow International Film Festival. Suddenly Moscow was the *in* place to be. Russia was chic. Movie stars from around the world flocked to Red Square. Gorbachev became a media star, taking the spotlight away from Ronald Reagan, who was mired in the mess of Iran-Contra.

The festival was organized by the Soviet State Committee on Cinematography (Goskino) and its subsidiary, Sovinfilm. "No wonder our trip fell through," I said to Richard. "For Sovinfilm, arranging a camping tour for museum research associates to watch nomads in the boondocks was all pain and no gain compared to arranging five-star hotels for international celebrities to watch movies in Moscow."

We went to Richard's beach house in Mexico to rest and relax. Every day the Chief took long walks on the beach, doing what he enjoyed most—thinking.

12

One afternoon he staggered in and plopped down on the large sofa chair in the living room. "I'm a real hero, man," he said, exhausted.

"I know that, Chief; what makes you say that right now?"

"I just saved a Mexican boy, and two men who had gone in after him, from drowning." I couldn't imagine how the Chief, who had undergone his third major surgery for cancer only nine months before (and for years had been dogged by an irregular pulse and high blood pressure), could have survived such an ordeal. The waters at Playa de la Misión, on the "Pacific" coast, are anything but peaceful.

"But that's not the worst of it," he continued. "To thank me, the women on the beach gave me some raw mussels in hot sauce. I thought I'd never be able to keep it down."

When we returned to Pasadena, a letter was waiting for me. Lamin reported that the local visa office could not process our visas until after he returned from Japan. (He was to visit Osaka for two months with another Soviet exhibition.) Our "second sledge" was on hold.

A few weeks later Richard and I went to see Dr. Keller and Professor Gary Seaman of USC to discuss upcoming events. Professor Seaman was organizing a workshop for the end of September to coordinate plans for the exhibition, its symposium, and a festival of documentary films on nomads of Eurasia. Seaman's idea was to have Owen Lattimore and Richard Feynman as honorary chairmen of the workshop (what a meeting of remarkable men *that* would be!), with Kapitsa and Basilov representing the Soviet Academy of Sciences, and Surikov representing Sovinfilm. If everything went well—that is, Surikov got his trip to Disneyland—we could revive the planning trip and go to Tuva in October.

I suggested also inviting Maxim Munzuk to the conference. "Maybe Munzuk would have enough pull to get us into Tuva himself," I said. "At least he could see Hollywood and tour the Academy of Motion Picture Arts and Sciences, which gave *Dersu Uzala* the Oscar that he probably never saw."

"That's fine with me," said Dr. Keller. "But Kapitsa has already requested that his wife come along, and the Museum has agreed to pay for her airfare—that's another first-class ticket to Los Angeles. Besides, Kapitsa and Basilov have asked us three or four times to reissue their invitation—it keeps getting lost every step of the way. I don't see how someone off in Tuva stands a chance."

We tried anyway, but Keller was right: Munzuk was unable to accept our invitation. Surikov begged off, saying he had prior commitments.

As September approached, the Museum got in touch with Los Angeles County's protocol department. The Kapitsas and Basilov would be chauffeured around Los Angeles in a special limousine; their engagements included a special welcoming ceremony at the County Board of Supervisors, several posh dinner parties, and, of course, shopping in Beverly Hills.

Richard's idea was to entertain the Kapitsas not as VIPs, but as regular people. He offered to have them stay in his home (Basilov would stay with some neighbors), and to take them camping—to show the Vice-President of the Academy of Sciences how we preferred to travel in Tuva.

The Museum got rooms for its distinguished guests at the Bel Air Hotel, tucked away among the finest residential real estate in Los Angeles.

The Soviets arrived in Los Angeles on a Saturday night, and were met by Dr. Keller at the airport. Immediately it became clear why Article 21 of the protocol specified, "For the official delegation of the Academy of Sciences of the USSR the hotel and airplane tickets must be first class": Kapitsa's girth was at least fifty inches!

Pyotr Kapitsa, Andrei's father, had won the 1978 Nobel

prize in physics for his research in the 1930s.[1] Andrei's first request was for Dr. Keller to help him obtain money by wire from a certain Swedish bank account.

While the Kapitsas relaxed at their hotel on Sunday, I showed Basilov around Los Angeles. As we cruised the diverse ethnic neighborhoods, I could see Vladimir was impatient: he wanted to fulfill his goal of swimming off the eastern shores of the Pacific (he had already swum in the waters near Vladivostok), so we headed for Venice Beach and took a dip in polluted Santa Monica Bay.

That night, the Soviets were entertained by Natural History Museum director Dr. Black and his wife, Dr. Black. (His wife also has a Ph.D.)

The following day, Monday, the Kapitsas were shown around the studio of the famous gem photographers Harold and Erica Van Pelt. Meanwhile, Basilov went to the Museum and began discussions about the exhibition.

That evening it was the Feynmans' turn to entertain the Soviets. Following the Museum's example, Gweneth hired two high-class caterers, got out her best silver, and prepared all day for the spread. In the late afternoon I drove out to the Bel Air Hotel in Phoebe's parents' car. (Mine was too small, and lacked air conditioning.) I knocked on Basilov's door, waking him from a deep sleep. As Vladimir got dressed, I went next door to summon the Kapitsas.

The Vice-President of the Soviet Academy of Sciences was dressed in an old short-sleeve shirt that could have come from a 1960s K-Mart. Looking at my white shirt and the tie draped around my neck, Kapitsa said, "Do you think Professor Feynman would object if we dressed informally tonight?"

"Not at all," I replied happily. I quickly telephoned the Chief and told him the good news.

---

[1]The summary in the *Encyclopaedia Britannica* (15th ed.) of the elder Kapitsa's remarkable life is well worth reading.

Basilov soon appeared—in coat and tie—and we drove to Pasadena. On the way, we talked a little about Tuva. I was tempted to say, "Why did you push us over to Sovinfilm?" but held my tongue: maybe Kapitsa would personally help get us to Tuva—now that he had made it to California himself. That would depend on how well he hit it off with Richard. Emboldened by Kapitsa's wearing such a tacky shirt, I mentioned Feynman's desire to visit Tuva as an ordinary person rather than as a VIP.

Kapitsa smiled. "To protect his identity, we could issue Feynman a visa under the name of Fenimore Cooper," he said, noting the similarity in names between the Chief and the American writer (whom I had never heard of, I was embarrassed to admit).

The evening went wonderfully. To Gweneth's delight, Kapitsa held forth with tall tales about expeditions to Africa and Antarctica, adventures in Alaska (where he served as a consultant to the consortium building the Alaska pipeline), and his visit to a permafrost institute in—of all places—Arizona. For once it was Feynman saying "Really?" and "Incredible!"

Andrei and Richard immediately became friends. They discussed matters of all kinds, including Richard's unpleasant experiences in Italy and Poland with Soviet science delegations packed with KGB agents.

"The Academy of Sciences used to be run by the Moscow Mafia," Andrei said. "But it is better now. We got rid of the KGB."

I noted that although Brezhnev had sent Sakharov into exile in Gorky, the Academy of Sciences had always kept Sakharov in their ranks, paying him his monthly pension and keeping his apartment and dacha open for his return.

Still, Feynman was uncomfortable with the idea of visiting Moscow and meeting scientists officially, even after visiting Tuva. "But there are some individual scientists whose work I am quite interested in," he said.

"You could meet with them privately," replied Andrei. "Ralph told me how you want to visit Tuva incognito. We have even discussed issuing you a visa under the name of Fenimore Cooper!"

The Chief loved the idea. Everyone smiled—even Basilov, who was on the edge of falling back into his deep sleep.

As I drove the Soviets back to their hotel, I asked what they wanted to see in California—perhaps Yosemite National Park?

"I have always wanted to see Yosemite," said Andrei. "We would be very, very happy if we could go there."

"I'll talk to the Museum and try to arrange it," I replied.

"We would also like to see Oakland," said Andrei.

"Oakland? I don't know of anything in Oakland but Jack London Square."

"That's exactly what we would like to see. Jack London is very popular in the Soviet Union."

"I can understand that," I said, trying to recover from my earlier embarrassing disclosure of ignorance. "I read *The Call of the Wild* when I was in high school."

The next day I telephoned the Soviet Desk at the State Department, and found out it was okay to take the Soviets anywhere in the United States as long as we said where we were going. So I called the Museum and got approval to take the Kapitsas to Yosemite and Oakland.

The next day Dr. Keller and I showed the Soviets around Disneyland. Andrei recorded everything on his Sony Video 8 camera, which he had purchased in Japan on a recent trip. As we discussed video systems, Andrei relayed a request by his brother Sergei, the host of a popular science program on television for young people in the USSR: find a converter for his satellite dish antenna so he could receive channels on the new Ku band. The Kapitsas regularly watched U.S. and Western European stations, recording the BBC and other services on their multi-system video recorders. (I found a converter two days later.)

On Friday everyone went over to USC to attend the workshop organized by Professor Seaman. Unfortunately, Owen Lattimore could not attend: he had suffered a stroke a few weeks after his interview with André Singer, and couldn't speak. Thus Richard Feynman was alone as honorary chairman of the workshop. His opening remarks, delivered at a working breakfast, briefly recounted the improbable events which led to that international gathering. (They appear as Appendix B.)

As Dr. Keller was delivering his own words of welcome, Basilov, who sat to my left, leaned over and asked me to do him a favor: in Russian etiquette, when one is addressing another person respectfully, one uses the first and middle names, not the last name. For example, he addressed Kapitsa, his boss, as "Andrei Petrovich." Basilov had forgotten Mrs. Kapitsa's middle name, and was too embarrassed to ask her what it was. As an American, I could address her as "Mrs. Kapitsa" without being impolite.

"Mrs. Kapitsa," I said, "I was interested to know your middle name."

"Oh, that's all right," she replied. "You can just call me Eugenia—or Zhenia, if you prefer."

I laughed inside, thinking of Basilov's frustration over his stymied plan. But I thought I'd better try to help him, so I said, "Thank you, Eugenia. I know your husband's middle name is Petrovich; I was just interested to know how it works in a woman's case."

"My middle name is Alexandrovna," she said. "My father's name was Alexander."

"I see," I said, winking at Basilov, who gave only the slightest hint of a nod.

After the breakfast was over, the workshop participants

went across the street to the Museum. The Chief was rather tired, so I took him home.

That evening there was a formal reception for the workshop participants at the Blacks' home. There was female valet parking, entertainment by a balalaika duo, and plenty of caviar, blintzes, and other Russian delicacies—not to mention the copious amounts of vodka and other alcoholic fare. Among the many gifts bestowed upon the guests of honor was a gaudy "Key to the County."

The international finder of museum exhibitions enjoys a glass of ice water with his assistant at a reception for Soviet VIPs. (Courtesy Natural History Museum of Los Angeles County.)

Richard spent nearly the whole evening talking with Professor Li Youyi of the Chinese Academy of Social Sciences about Chinese history and science. The Chief had been interested in how the Chinese had progressed so far in science so early, but then became bogged down in superstition. He had read quite a lot on the subject, to Dr. Li's delight.

They also talked about Tuva. Dr. Li said there were a few thousand Tuvans living in the Altai, in the far north of Sinkiang near the border with Mongolia, and was confident that he could arrange a trip there for us. When Richard told me the news, I said, "Good! The Tuvans in Sinkiang are probably less corrupted by outsiders than the Tuvans in Tuva. And on our way north from Ürümchi, we can stop off and put up a monument to the *real* center of Asia."[2]

As Phoebe and I prepared to leave the reception, I asked the Kapitsas if they preferred to attend the workshop at USC the next day, or see some sights in Los Angeles. The answer was emphatic: they wanted to see some sights—in particular, the J. Paul Getty Museum.

I knew that normally one must make a reservation to enter the Getty Museum, whose galleries are housed in a replica of a Roman Villa built on top of a parking lot. So when I picked up the Kapitsas the next day, I asked them to bring their "Key to the County."

When we arrived at the Getty Museum, the guard asked for my name. I said, "Leighton."

"I don't see your name on the reservation list, Mr. Leighton," he said.

"I didn't have time to make a reservation," I said. "The visitors asked me only last night if they could see your excellent museum. They're from the USSR, and will be in Los Angeles only a few days."

[2]In case you missed it, see Footnote 4 on page 80.

"I'm sorry, but without a reservation, you cannot enter."

I pulled out the gaudy key from its ceremonial box. "Would this help?" I asked.

"Go ahead," said the guard, with obvious displeasure. "Just tell the Russians to make peace."

Kapitsa laughed.

The next day all the workshop participants were given a tour of Santa Catalina, an island twenty-five miles southwest of Los Angeles, where USC had a research station. The boat trip took ninety minutes across choppy waters. The sun broke through the clouds as we disembarked and approached the restaurant for our prearranged lunch.

We couldn't help but notice a boisterous group of men sitting out on a large, wooden deck sipping beer. To a man, every one of them was dressed in cowboy clothes—hat, chaps, boots, spurs—just like in the movies. But when I overheard their conversations, I was flabbergasted: rather than calf-roping or lassoing, the talk was about interest rates, real estate, and the latest investments on Wall Street!

There were a couple of special characters among these urban cowboys. One was a mustachioed Mexican-American, proud of his heritage, wearing a large sombrero—just like Pancho Villa. The other, an old geezer who looked like he had just finished a hard day of prospecting, was holding forth with some crazy story that had everyone in stitches when suddenly he saw the Chief and said, "Hey, Dick!"

Richard's face lit up. "Zorth!" he cried. It was Jirayr Zorthian, the eccentric Altadena artist Richard had known for years.

The encounter couldn't have been better if it had been staged.

As Kapitsa happily took videos of these remnants of American nomadic culture, Basilov posed stiffly with a wasted cowboy who kissed him on the cheek. The politically conservative

cowboys immediately became citizen diplomats, pulling deco-
rations off their hats to trade. The Stetsons of a half-dozen
members of Los Caballeros are now adorned with pins from
the USSR Academy of Sciences.

The Invitation Arrives

13 ON the way back from Catalina Island, Andrei Kapitsa promised he would personally see to it that the USSR Academy of Sciences arranged a trip to Tuva for Richard, Glen, and me—plus Gweneth Feynman, Phoebe Kwan, and Thomas Luehrsen. He asked each of us to write down our full name and date of birth; we could send him a detailed wish list of Tuva sights later. We would travel in May or June 1988.

As Richard was still fatigued from the day at Catalina, he bowed out of the trip to Yosemite and Oakland. Gweneth, too, stayed home—sensing that her husband's health was not good.

When Phoebe and I returned to Los Angeles, we found out that Richard had undergone cancer surgery—for the fourth time. But the Chief was already well on the road to recovery: a young doctor had tried a new technique—giving an epidural injection of pain killers—that enabled Richard to breathe unhindered despite the trauma to his abdomen, thus avoiding the usual complications, including pneumonia. Within a week he was out of the hospital.

A day or two later we received a letter—written on a Tuvan typewriter—from our longtime correspondent Ondar Daryma:

Dear Ralph,

How living are you? Special-interest what is? [What's new?] Tuva-to when come you? Who-all come-will? . . . When coming, you Tuva's nice corners-to take we. From there thither you self-my's family-with, friends-with meet will. Tuva's hot springs, historic grounds, herders (horse, yak, camels, . . .), and hunters bring we. . . .

You personal friends-with Tuva concerning color movie-picture taking well-known accomplished? It this summer's end, autumn's beginning-in done could-be good. . . . [It seemed Ondar had heard of our film planning trip, and thought it might still be on!]

Mister Richard Feynman-to, Glen Cowan-to, and your family-to Big River's (Yenisei's) source-from warm greetings filling am I. You-to steel-like strong health, happiness, long life, peace for the sake of all sides-with successes be yours wish I.

Road-to good brings coming-your wish we!

Meeting-to greetings! Big-with [thanks] filled-am-I!

Daryma Ondar Kish-Chalaevich.

Inspired by Ondar's words, the Chief took daily walks with his friend from Kyzyl to Shagonar, then to Chadan, and eventually all the way to Teeli, this time imagining that our pen pal was introducing us to hunters and herders along the way. Within weeks, Richard was teaching again at Caltech.

Meanwhile, Dr. Keller had accompanied the Soviets to Denver (the next stop on the Nomads tour), and to Washington, D.C., where the exhibition would finish at the Smith-sonian in early 1990. Upon his return, Keller was fuming: Kapitsa had insisted on receiving his per diem money early—in cash—from Keller's own pocket. Although Keller would be compensated for the funds later, Kapitsa's brutish behavior added insult to injury: he had not notified the Bel Air Hotel of his trip to Yosemite and Oakland, thus sticking the Mu-seum with an extra four nights of hotel expenses—in addition to several $150 meals ordered in his room.

To top it off, an FBI agent dropped in unexpectedly and interrogated Keller about the Vice-President of the USSR Academy of Sciences visiting Oakland, site of an army depot and a large supply center for the navy. Although I reminded Keller that the State Department had said everything was okay, the FBI was not assuaged.

Nevertheless, from our point of view, Kapitsa had given us our firmest assurance yet that we would go to Tuva—at the expense of the Academy of Sciences, no less!

In early November Phoebe and I received a letter from Lamin, who had since returned from Japan. Our official docu-ments were enclosed: we could go to Novosibirsk and on to Tuva anytime before January 27, 1988. If we wanted to go in the summer of 1988, we should begin the application proce-dure again immediately.

Because we had received Kapitsa's word that we would all go to Tuva together, I politely declined Lamin's offer for the winter of 1987–88. But I said that if Kapitsa's promised trip fell through, Phoebe and I would gladly visit Novosibirsk in the summer of 1988.

On December 7, 1987, I received the following telegram:

PRELIMINARY DECISION OF YOUR INVITATION IS DONE. DR. BASILOV VISITED TUVA AND MET PEO-PLE CONNECTED WITH THE PROGRAM. I HOPE DURING DECEMBER YOU WILL RECEIVE OFFICIAL

INVITATION . . . BEST WISHES AND GOOD HEALTH
FOR RICHARD.

BEST REGARDS TO MM. FEYNMAN AND FEBE.

KAPITSA

After sending our thanks to Andrei and Eugenia, I called
Chris Sykes. "If you want to talk to us before we know we're
going for sure, you'd better come soon."

Sykes replied, "I still haven't found any money for filming,
but I'll come out anyway, shortly after the New Year."

Meanwhile, just before Christmas, I received a letter (in
Russian) from Tuva:

Dear Ralph,

A colleague of Daryma from Kyzyl is writing you. He
showed me your letters. I had a conversation with Vainshtein,
who said that my film, Songs of Tuva, will be shown at this
exhibition. I would like to know about this exhibition. Write
if you can.

I'm busy studying Tuvan folk music, and I'm investigating
throat singing. Not long ago, an ethnomusicologist from the
US came, Theodore Levin, with photographer Karen Sherlock from Wisconsin. With them I collected a lot of materials,
and we're going to put out a joint record, USSR-USA.[1]

I take advantage of this chance to wish you a Merry Christmas.

Zoya Kyrgysovna Kyrgys

I remembered Levin from way back in 1982, in connection
with David Hykes and the Harmonic Choir. Levin had made
it to Tuva, at last!

[1]This record (as well as tape and CD) is called Tuva: Voices from the Center of Asia,
and came out in 1990 under the Smithsonian/Folkways label (catalog listing SF-
40017). It is available from Roundup Records, Box 154, North Cambridge, MA
01240, or through Friends of Tuva (see Appendix C).

I telephoned him and asked how he had done it. Levin had extensive contacts in Moscow, developed from arranging concert tours for American musicians in the USSR. He was a member of the Soviet musicians union, and had a bank account in rubles. I thought, For once, some Americans were able to reach Tuva via Moscow.

Levin said the Tuvans were not yet accustomed to foreigners, and had literally repainted the hotel in downtown Kyzyl for him and Sherlock. Everywhere they went it was like a Potemkin village: everything was arranged; nothing was spontaneous. "We plan to return next summer," he said. "I think we'll be able to get into remote areas this time, now that we've broken the ice on the first trip."

I asked why he took a photographer. "We're preparing an article for the *National Geographic,*" he said. (I found out later that Levin suffered the same fate as we did: he got bumped by a *Geographic* staff writer whose article was on a neighboring region—this time it was Siberia.)

At the end of January, 1988, Chris Sykes came out from London to interview Richard. The Chief was often tired and occasionally depressed. But when he began talking about Tuva, his malaise disappeared. His face lit up, his eyes sparkled, his enthusiasm for life was infectious. Between episodes of storytelling we beat out some old, familiar rhythms on our drums.[2] It seemed obvious to everyone around him that Richard's discomfort and depression were psychological.

Nevertheless, two days after Sykes finished filming, the Chief went to see his internist. "Even if it is psychological, it won't hurt to run some tests," said Dr. Kim.

[2]This interview became "The Quest for Tannu Tuva" on the BBC, and "Last Journey of a Genius" on PBS. I am trying to obtain the home video rights for it and for Sykes's other Feynman interview, "The Pleasure of Finding Things Out," from the BBC as another fund raiser for the John Wayne Cancer Clinic at UCLA. Please write to Friends of Tuva for details (see Appendix C).

When the results came back, Dr. Kim said, "Professor Feynman, you'd better go out to UCLA . . ."

Less than a week later, the Chief's borrowed time had run out. He died on February 15—which, as it happened, was Mardi Gras in 1988. I imagined the rhythmist's spirit stopping off in Rio for a night of *Carnaval* on its way to that special place in our hearts.

News of Feynman's death was slow to reach Moscow. In early March Gweneth received a letter dated February 19, 1988. The letterhead was adorned with two busts of Lenin. The text said:

Dear Professor R. P. Feynman,

I have the great pleasure to invite you, your wife, and four of your colleagues to visit the Soviet Union as the guests of the USSR Academy of Sciences.

I was informed by the corresponding member of the USSR Academy of Sciences, Prof. A. P. Kapitsa, that you would like to visit Tuva ASSR and get acquainted with its sightseeings. We consider the most favourable time for such a trip to be the period of May and June of this year. Your trip will take three to four weeks.

I hope that during your tour you will have time to meet Soviet colleagues in Novosibirsk and Moscow who know your activities and works and, undoubtedly, will be very pleased to meet you.

Kindly note that the USSR Academy of Sciences will cover expenses on your and your colleagues' staying in the USSR.

Yours sincerely,

Academician E. P. Velikhov

Epilogue

LIKE Magellan, Richard Feynman completed his last journey in our minds and hearts. Through his inspiration to others, his dream took on a life of its own.

The Tuva story continues, even as I am writing now. It is difficult to know where to end this rendition of it, so I will summarize some of the major points:

> Vainshtein encouraged the rest of us to accept the Academy's invitation. But when we notified Velikhov and Kapitsa repeatedly of our desire to visit Tuva, our messages went unanswered. I heard from Basilov later that a new invitation would have to be drawn up. (It never was.)
>
> Phoebe and I decided to accept Lamin's personal invitation to visit Novosibirsk in June. We went by way of Japan, stopping in Nara to see Vainshtein at the huge $82 million Silk

14

Road exposition there, before puddle-jumping to Novosibirsk via Niigata, Khabarovsk, and Bratsk. After three days
of calling in chips from his many friends in the Party,
Lamin—one of Nixon's hosts on his 1959 "Kitchen Debate" trip to the Soviet Union—succeeded in procuring us
permission to visit Kyzyl, plus the plane tickets to get there.
It was a harrowing process—not so much the bureaucratic
maneuvering, but Lamin's driving: as we careened through
streets jammed with pedestrians, Lamin honked his horn and
shook his fist at the scurrying masses, barely missing babies
and *babushkas* alike. I surmised that no ordinary citizen could
ever get a high Party official prosecuted for manslaughter, if it
came to that.

We flew over the Sayan Mountains in a small jet called a
Yak 40, filled with students returning home to Tuva for the
summer. My phrasebook Tuvan was actually understood
over the engine noise by a Tuvan girl who asked me (in
Russian) what time it was.

Our activities in Tuva included: watching yaks, camels,
and reindeer—in a propaganda film; admiring the familiar
buildings of downtown Kyzyl, including the new government building (minus the car in front); meeting various
local personalities, who used the occasion to readjust the
local pecking order; visiting a Young Pioneer Camp (where
we received the same celebrity attention that smothered
Samantha Smith); and passing several yurts used by shepherds—so we could be entertained by a politician in a yurt
set up specifically for our visit. We were seeing the world
the way the Vice-President does: had I not pored so long
over every map and book I could find about Tuva, I might
have thought we had actually seen the place![1]

[1] If my descriptions of our activities sound too brief, it is because our inaugural trip
was distorted much like Ted Levin's was: although the hotel in downtown Kyzyl did
not smell of yet another coat of fresh paint, there was still the pervasive atmosphere
of a Potemkin village. A more accurate and complete description of Tuva today must
await another trip and another book.

Accompanied by our pen pal, Ondar Daryma, we went by boat up the Yenisei River to Toora Khem and then by bus to Lake Azas, a new resort whose evening entertainment for Tuvan youth consisted of Bruce Lee movies on video dubbed into English and then into Russian. Walking in the nearby woods, we descended from the main trail to a mineral spring. Handkerchiefs and strips of cloth—reminiscent of Armenia and Korea—adorned the bushes and trees nearby. Ondar silently prayed to the local spirits before drinking the curative water.

Back in Kyzyl we stood before our Holy Grail, the monument to the "Centre of Asia." It seemed like Richard's grave.

Another moment of heartache came when we were shown into the Kyzyl Drama Theater, where the Chief and I had dreamed of playing drums. Dominating the lower floor of the white marble foyer was an intriguing contraption seemingly made just for the Chief: copper bowls and chains led water down alternate paths in a slow, regular pattern—it was a water clock.

In the upstairs foyer we were treated to an informal folk music program by local artists, which included drumming—a shaman's dance—and several renditions of throat singing. One number featured "Dersu Uzala" himself (Maxim Munzuk) and his wife singing a ditty akin to "There's a Hole in the Bucket, Dear Liza" in Tuvan. After the program I shook Munzuk's hand, turned to the other performers and spectators, and recited a certain flowery Tuvan phrase that was already familiar to him: "From the depths of my soul I greet you, wish you success in your work, good health, and happiness in your life!"

Everyone smiled and applauded. I was thankful they didn't say anything back, for I certainly would not have understood it.

We visited Ondar and his family (wife, daughter, son, daughter-in-law, and grandson) in their modest apartment. The phrase "How many rooms are there in your apartment?" came to mind, as well as the answer: "I have a comfortable apartment." There was indeed a housing shortage in Kyzyl.

Ondar serenaded us with Tuvan songs as his wife served us fat of lamb's tail. After showing us the letters, books, and photograph—the one taken at our wedding—that he had received from far-away California, Ondar presented us with a stone carving of a bull he had made himself. From his many talents and extensive knowledge of folklore, Daryma appeared to be on a one-man crusade to preserve Tuvan culture. It was understandable, now, why he had responded to and encouraged our attempts to communicate in Tuvan.

When Phoebe and I visited Ondar's institute, the TNIIYaLI, someone asked us why we were visiting Tuva. I resorted to the official-sounding explanation that the Nomads exhibition, which contained many Tuvan artifacts, was going to California—a complete revelation to the Tuvans: as on earlier occasions, when the exhibition had gone to Japan, Finland, and Sweden (always accompanied by officials from Moscow and Leningrad), the Academy of Sciences had simply commandeered the materials from Tuva and from local museums throughout the USSR without saying they would be going abroad.

As we were leaving, someone from the institute pressed into my hand the address of a Russian colonist who had left Kyzyl in 1929, and who was now living in Bell—less than ten miles from downtown Los Angeles. So there *was* someone from Tuva living in California—the only problem was, she was too old to drive, and thus never had a chance to see the TOUVA license plate on my car.

British anthropologist Dr. Caroline Humphrey also succeeded in reaching Tuva that summer. She made a film called *Herders of Möngün Taiga* for Granada Television in the U. K. Meanwhile, Dr. Basilov was showing the Natural History Museum's director and his friends around Leningrad, Moscow, Turkmenia, and Uzbekistan—on a free trip provided under the protocol. For some reason or other, Basilov ended up just as mad at Keller's boss as Keller had been with Basilov's boss.

On November 9, 1988, Tuva made the front page of the *Christian Science Monitor* in an article called "Perestroika in the Provinces." (Tuva was in the news again—this time in newspapers around the world—in the summer and fall of 1990, when a series of anti-Russian riots took place.)

On February, 4, 1989, "Nomads: Masters of the Eurasian Steppe" opened at the Natural History Museum in Los Angeles. Media coverage—including a full-page spread in *Time*—perpetuated the myth that big shots meet and then everything falls magically into place. Reality was rudely different: Dr. Basilov was not accorded a reception by the Museum's director upon his arrival, as the Swedes had provided us in Göteborg; instead, he was put right to work in the trenches. Basilov worked with such intensity that by the time he was finished, he had rearranged—to the chagrin of the Museum's designers—the contents of all the museum cases.

The catalog for the exhibition, *Nomads of Eurasia,* was translated by Mary Fleming Zirin, who by then was a translator with a superior reputation.[2] The Acoustiguide tour of the exhibition was narrated by Omar Sharif (chosen because of his role as Genghis Khan, though most people remembered him as Dr. Zhivago); his illuminating script was written by one of the clowns from California. Richard's hearty laugh at such delightful absurdity in the world reverberated through my head.

The logo for the exhibition was the big bronze plaque from Scythian times depicting a coiled panther—the one Vainshtein told us he had excavated in Tuva. Also featured was the exquisite golden finial depicting a wild boar biting a hunter, whose dog was biting the boar—the one that Richard had read about in the *Los Angeles Times* eleven years before.

An unexpected member of the visiting Soviet delegation was Dr. Yuri Aranchyn, director of the Tuvan Scientific Research Institute of Language, Literature, and History. He was the first Tuvan to visit California. Unlike the rest of the Soviet delegation, he did not buy a video recorder with the dollars he received from the Museum under the protocol; instead, he bought his wife a rabbit fur coat from France. (Furs—in the past extracted by Chinese overlords and Mongol princes as tribute, and today "often rank first at international auctions," according to *Soviet Life*—evidently are not readily available in Tuva.) On a shopping tour in the garment district, the cosmopolitan character of Los Angeles became especially evident: as I was naming prices in Tuvan to Dr. Aranchyn, a shopkeeper said to me, "You speak Turk-

[2]Most recently she had translated and annotated *The Cavalry Maiden* by Nadezhda Durova, published by Indiana University Press in 1988. Her translation and the book itself have received excellent reviews; the story might become a major motion picture.

ish? I come from Azerbaijan, Iran."[3] Later, an African man standing on a street corner selling luggage overheard the Soviets in conversation. He addressed them—in Russian, which he had learned at Patrice Lumumba University in Moscow.

Shopping was not easy for some of the visitors. One elderly Muscovite summed up the superpowers' respective economic conditions perfectly with her limited English: "In Soviet Union, not enough stuff—big problem. In United States, too much stuff—big problem!"

Christian Axel-Nilsson and his wife came to Los Angeles from Sweden to see the exhibition. (It was their first trip to the United States.) I drove them and Aranchyn to San Francisco via Solvang (a Danish settlement near Ronald Reagan's ranch) and Esalen (keeping a respectful distance from the bathing nudes), where Aranchyn was pleased to see a yurt. As he peered inside, I wondered whether any of the participants sitting on pillows dared imagine where the visitor came from—Mongolia, perhaps?

Basilov finally got to experience Esalen himself, in a seminar on shamanism he conducted jointly with guru Michael Harner of New York.

Lamin missed out on coming to Los Angeles—perhaps it was his place that was given to the Tuvan, Aranchyn, as it was Lamin who brought to Tuva the people who spilled the beans about the exhibition going to California. Lamin didn't lose out completely, however: he ended up going to Denver, where he gave a useless talk on the condition of nomads in the Soviet Union today.

[3]Turkish is spoken in Azerbaijan, which straddles the Soviet-Iranian border. Turkic languages are spoken from Istanbul to Baku, Samarkand, Kyzyl, and beyond.

After visiting California in June, 1989 (on a private invitation), a Tuvan arranged for Gweneth Feynman, Glen
Cowan, and others to visit Tuva (also on a private invitation) in the summer of 1990. But on December 31, 1989,
Gweneth died of cancer.

In November, 1989, Phoebe and I went to Washington,
D.C., and attended the opening of "Nomads" at the

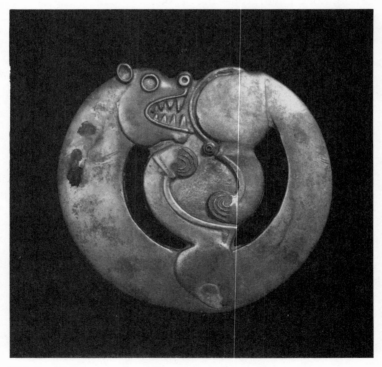

This Scythian bronze plaque from the eighth century B.C. became the logo
for the exhibition *Nomads: Masters of the Eurasian Steppe.* The plaque—
made with leather straps on its back side, to be worn by a horse—was
excavated in Tuva. (Courtesy Natural History Museum of Los Angeles
County. Photo by Dana Levy.)

Smithsonian's National Museum of Natural History. (It turned out that the American botanist who visited Tuva with Elias and Murray—the one named Stanwyn Shetler, whom I was unable to trace—worked at that museum.) Also present were Ted Levin and Professor Krueger, author of the *Tuvan Manual.* Plans for further contacts with Tuva were discussed, and continue to unfold: Levin proposed a throat-singing conference in Kyzyl to mark the Chief's seventy-fifth birthday (May, 1993); Krueger has been invited to visit the TNIIYaLI to write a Tuvan-English phrasebook; and a contingent of throat-singing Tuvan horsemen may yet appear on New Year's Day in the Tournament of Roses Parade.

Professor William A. Shear of Hampden-Sydney College has named a species of milliped discovered in the mountains of Tuva *Diplomaragna feynmani.*

The mystery of the eccentric English traveler who erected the original monument to the "Centre of Asia" is one step closer to solution: according to a Tuvan source, his name was Dr. Proctor.

Ralph and Alan Leighton have been invited by Dr. Aranchyn to travel extensively throughout Tuva in the summer of 1991 with the purpose of writing about it.

Plans are afoot by Friends of Tuva to place a memorial plaque to Richard Feynman in Kyzyl's monument to the "Centre of Asia."

Appendix A

HERE is Glen Cowan's translation of the protocol that brought the exhibition "Nomads of Eurasia" to the United States. Comments of the author appear in brackets.

Protocol

of negotiations between representatives of the Academy of Sciences of the USSR, hereinafter called the Soviet side, and the Natural History Museum of Los Angeles County, hereinafter called the American side.

Place and time of exhibition:

1. Los Angeles, Museum of Natural History;
2. Area of exhibition: 1100 square meters;
3. Time of exhibition: from January 15 through April 15, 1989.

The Soviet Side:

1. Organizes in Los Angeles (USA) the exhibition "Nomadic Peoples of Eurasia" from collections of scientific organizations of the Academy of Sciences of the USSR and from separate museums of the USSR. The collection of exhibited items will be enlarged in comparison with the exhibition already carried out in Sweden;

2. Develops a thematic-expositional plan of the exhibition "Nomadic Peoples of Eurasia" and presents it to the American side (in Russian) not later than December 31, 1987, for translation into English;

3. Will present not later than December 31, 1987, a list of items to be exhibited in Russian and will provide information on their insurance value [the list came one year late];

4. Incurs the cost in Soviet rubles for the preparation of the exhibition in the USSR;

5. Provides and pays for in Soviet rubles transportation of the exhibition cargo from Moscow to New York and back;

6. Will send to the American side information about the contents and weight of the exhibition cargo before December 31, 1987 [again, the information came one year late, by telephone—and it didn't match the contents of the cargo];

7. Sends to the USA:

7.1 Two representatives of the Soviet side for work on preparation of the exhibition in 1988 for a period of three weeks;

7.2 The director of the exhibition for its entire duration, and five specialists for work at the exhibition for a period of three months each;

7.3 Two specialists for assembly and disassembly of the exhibition for a total period of twenty-four days (fourteen days for assembly and ten days for disassembly), returning to the Soviet Union each time;

7.4 An official delegation of the Academy of Sciences of the USSR consisting of five persons for participation in the opening ceremony of the exhibition for a period of ten days each;

7.5 Two specialists for participation in a symposium for a period of ten days each;

8. Will receive at its own expense from the USA a delegation of two specialists in 1988 for work on preparation of the exhibition in the USSR, including carrying out photographic work, for a period of three weeks;

9. Carries out the assembly, maintenance, and disassembly of the exhibition, in accordance with the established periods of time, with the help of the American specialists;

10. Submits before December 31, 1987, the text (in Russian) and necessary illustration materials for a catalog [these materials arrived only six months late];

11. Submits before December 31, 1987, color and black-and-white photographic materials for the mounting of the exhibition, and also recordings of musical works [again, one year late];

12. Gives explanations to the American visitors about the subjects of the exhibition;

13. Organizes lectures about the subjects of the exhibition;

14. Will send to the exhibition scientific and popular films about the subjects of the exhibition;

15. Provides insurance for the exhibited items through "Ingosstrakh," the insurance joint-stock company of the USSR, in the established manner for the period of time while the exhibition cargo is located in the USSR and during transportation from Moscow to New York and back;

16. Will pay for transportation of all Soviet specialists from Moscow to New York and back.

The American Side:

1. Provides free of charge an exhibition hall for the carrying out of the exhibition "Nomadic Peoples of Eurasia"; provides at its own expense the necessary service personnel and services needed during the course of the exhibition;

2. Develops the design and provides the artistic scheme of the exhibition in accordance with the thematic-expositional plan and the provided exhibition hall; the design and artistic scheme must be agreed upon by the Soviet side [despite repeated attempts to get comments by Basilov on floor plans, etc., he never responded];

3. Will accept responsibility for the safety of the exhibited items and packing materials from the time of their arrival in the USA until their departure to Moscow and insures the exhibition cargo with "Ingosstrakh" through the firm "Lloyds" or an accepted equivalent;

4. Pays for transportation of the exhibition cargo and work connected with it in the territory of the USA;

5. Will receive at its own expense:

5.1 Two Soviet specialists for settling questions connected with the preparation of the exhibition in 1987 for a period of three weeks;

5.2 The director of the exhibition for its entire duration and five specialists for maintenance of the exhibition for a period of three months each;

5.3 Two specialists for assembly and disassembly of the exhibition for a total period of twenty-four days (fourteen days for assembly and ten days for disassembly), returning to the Soviet Union each time;

5.4 An official delegation of the Academy of Sciences of the USSR consisting of five persons for participation in the opening ceremony for a period of ten days each;

5.5 Two specialists for participation in a symposium for a period of ten days each;

5.6 Pays for the transportation of all Soviet specialists from New York to Los Angeles and back, and transport of 30 kilograms of additional baggage each [even that extra baggage wasn't enough to cover the cornucopia of consumer goods bought in the USA—see Number 21 below];

6. Will implement twenty-four-hour security for the exhibited items during the entire period of the exhibition;

7. Carries out and pays for assembly and disassembly of the exhibition;

8. Provides the exhibition with the necessary display cases, special stands, electrical fixtures, and lights at its own expense, and assembles the electrical equipment;

9. Will pay for the electricity used for lighting [what do they take us for, anyway?];

10. For display of gold and especially valuable objects provides display cases with specially developed, reliable security systems;

11. Implements fire prevention measures during the exhibition and during its assembly and disassembly;

12. Maintains the temperature of the exhibition hall between eighteen and twenty-four degrees Celsius and the humidity between 45 percent and 50 percent [in the Hermitage, they simply open the windows];

13. If necessary will carry out work connected with restoration of individual exhibited items [the Smithsonian came to regret a similar clause in its "Crossroads" exhibition], and also will carry out the restoration of items which are damaged during transport;

14. Will provide for the demonstration of scientific and popular films connected with the subjects of the exhibition on video displays in the exhibition hall;

15. Will provide for the playing of musical recordings in the exhibition hall;

16. Will carry out all design (printing, photographic, etc.) work in the exhibition at its own expense;

17. Will translate the thematic-expositional plan, the text of the catalog, and all texts concerning the design;

18. At its own expense publishes a catalog of the exhibition in the necessary quantity; produces the texts for the display cases, prints invitations, and develops and produces with the approval of the Academy of Sciences of the USSR an advertising poster;

18.1 Will provide for Soviet side free of cost 100 copies of the exhibition catalog, 50 advertising posters, and also 30 entrance tickets per month;

19. Provides for Soviet side a preliminary copy of the catalog;

20. Provides information about preliminary and ongoing events in connection with the exhibition to the press, radio, and television;

21. Will provide at its own expense hotel rooms or apartments with all conveniences and will pay a per diem of thirty dollars to all Soviet specialists coming to the USA in connection with the organizing and carrying out of the exhibition; [This is the most important clause for the Soviets. Five dollars goes to the Academy of Sciences (or to the host museum, now that *perestroika* is spreading); each individual gets to keep twenty-five dollars per day— supposedly for food and the like, but in reality for personal purchases such as video recorders!]

In the event that the value of the dollar should change, the indicated amount is to be adjusted proportionally; for the official delegation of the Academy of Sciences of the USSR the hotel and airplane tickets must be first class [for Kapitsa's large girth, and for the top of the Soviet pecking order];

22. Will provide in addition to the exhibition hall a room for the directorate and a room for the Soviet personnel of the exhibition with necessary furniture, dishes [for their canned provisions, as the Soviets were reluctant to

spend any of their per diem allowance on food], and a telephone;

23. Will provide at its own expense for the use of the directorate of the exhibition an automobile with a driver for the entire period of the exhibition or will pay for taxis; provides transportation for the Soviet specialists from the hotel and back [although the hotel was less than a mile away, the Soviets still wanted the car and driver];

24. Will pay for telephone calls for the directorate of the exhibition, including one call to Moscow per week; will pay postal expenses for the directorate of the exhibition;

25. Provides at its own expense newspapers in English for the [Soviet] employees of the exhibition [Basilov's personal request];

26. Organizes at its own expense for the Soviet specialists excursions and other cultural activities [that is, Disneyland and shopping];

27. In the case of necessity provides and pays for medical help for the Soviet specialists;

28. Organizes within the framework of the exhibition a Soviet-American symposium on ethnography and archaeology for a period of three days with the participation of the Soviet personnel working at the exhibition and also with the participation of two scientists invited from the USSR for ten days, at the expense of the American side; it is desirable that the symposium take place at the beginning of the exhibition, so that the participants can be present at the opening ceremony of the exhibition.

Additional Information:

1. Period of assembly—fourteen days; period of disassembly—ten days;

2. Programs for the carrying out of press conferences, the official opening ceremony, the subjects of lectures, and infor-

mation about films will be given additional examination and will require the agreement of representatives of both sides;

3. All questions arising during the preparation and carrying out of the exhibition will be decided at that time in a spirit of traditional friendship and mutual concern;

4. The Soviet side requests of the American side:

4.1 Not to open the exhibition cargo without a representative of the Academy of Sciences of the USSR;

4.2 To save the packing materials (while the items are being exhibited) in a dry place, and if they are damaged, to carry out the necessary repairs;

4.3 All work on the arrangement of the exhibited items during the exhibition and during assembly and disassembly (and also their packing for transport back to the USSR after the end of the exhibition) must be carried out only with the agreement of the Soviet director and in the presence of Soviet specialists;

4.4 All movements of the exhibited items must be carried out in the presence of the director of the exhibition; without the consent and presence of the Soviet director of the exhibition the display cases may not be opened;

5. The Soviet side, if there is an entrance fee for the exhibition, does not make any claims to payment from the sale of tickets or catalogs;

6. The American side protects the Soviet side from the claims of third parties in case of damage, destruction, and other insurance cases on the territory of the exhibition;

7. Production of copies of exhibited items, pictures, and photographs may be carried out by the American side only with the consent of the Soviet side, in an agreed-upon amount, and on the condition that a specially stipulated number of copies are to be submitted to the Soviet side;

8. The American side does not make any claims to analo-

gous reciprocal measures in the USSR, at least in connection with this exhibition;

9. Both sides agree to extend the present agreement if the
exhibition "Nomadic Peoples of Eurasia" can be shown in
other cities of the USA;

10. The American side will attempt to find the means to send
filmmakers for production of a documentary film on
themes connected with the subject matter of the exhibition. [Unfortunately, we failed to note that this was not a
guarantee that we would get to Tuva!]

This agreement is produced in copies, in Russian and
in English, both texts of which are equally authentic.

The agreement becomes effective from the moment of
its signing.

For the Soviet side: For the American side:

Representative of the Scientific   Director of the
Council for Exhibitions of the   Natural History Museum
Academy of Sciences of the USSR   of Los Angeles County
Professor A. P. Kapitsa   Dr. Craig C. Black

                                         Associate Director
                                         Public Programs
                                         Natural History Museum
                                         of Los Angeles County
                                         Dr. Peter S. Keller

Appendix B

HERE are Richard Feynman's remarks (slightly edited), delivered at the opening of the workshop for the exhibition "Nomads of Eurasia," held on September 25, 1987, at the University of Southern California.

Welcome

I'm especially delighted to welcome you to this workshop because I accidentally had something to do with all these fantastic effects which I had no intention of producing. I thought it would amuse you to know how it all began.

Ten years ago, my good friend Ralph Leighton was over at my house for dinner—he was a high school math teacher—and told me that he had just been given a class in geography.

I said, "What do you know about geography?"

241

He says, "Well, I listen to the shortwave radio . . ."

"All right," I said, "what ever happened to Tannu Tuva?"

Ralph knows me very well, and he knows that I can make up the name of a country just like that. So he said, "There's no such place."

But this time I was ahead, because there was such a place, and something happened to it.

When I was eleven years old I saved stamps—it was a very popular activity on our street in those days, and kids would run around with their Scott's catalog and approval sheets, and so forth—and one time I got some very lovely triangular and diamond-shaped stamps from a place called Tannu Tuva. My father showed me where it was—it was a little purple splotch northwest of Outer Mongolia. That was Tannu Tuva. It was an independent country.

When Ralph and I found it on the map, we saw it was now part of Russia. Then we saw the capital, Kyzyl, whose spelling was so strange and esoteric—having none of the conventional vowels in it—that we looked at each other and decided, "We must go to Tuva!"

That was ten years ago. To learn more about Tuva we made contact with everybody we could find who had ever heard of or knew anything about it. In particular we made contact with a Professor Vainshtein of the USSR Academy of Sciences' Institute of Ethnography, who had written books on the traditional culture and archaeology of Tuva.

Ralph visited Russia in 1985 and visited Vainshtein in Moscow. There he first learned of a USSR exhibition about nomadic peoples of the Eurasian steppe that included material from Tuva. (Vainshtein apparently had sent us catalogs about this exhibition, but we never received them.) The exhibition was going to go to Sweden in February, 1986.

So in February Ralph went to Sweden and saw the exhibition. (I couldn't go because I was in Washington serving on the Rogers Commission.) Ralph brought back a catalog and we thought, "This would be a good thing to bring to the United States."

The first contact we made was with the Los Angeles County Museum of Natural History. Dr. Keller fell immediately for the hook and thought the exhibition was a great idea. I sent a telegram to A. P. Kapitsa of the USSR Academy of Sciences, and soon Dr. Keller was in Moscow.

Because the Göteborg Historical Museum had given Ralph a copy of the protocol that brought the exhibition to Sweden, it was easy for Dr. Keller to make an agreement to bring an expanded version of the exhibition to the United States— one that includes, for the first time, a section on the Mongols.

So Ralph and I have been a sort of catalyst, producing a crystallization of supersaturated purposes: not only are people coming to see the exhibition, but scholars from the USA and the USSR are having a symposium at the University of Southern California,[1] and there will be public lectures and films on related topics. And so you can understand how it's a great delight for me to welcome you all here, to see a kind of reality resulting from the nonsense with which we began: we just wanted to visit what was to us the most esoteric, strange place in the world.

[1]Three volumes of the Proceedings of the Soviet-American Academic Symposia in Conjunction with the Museum Exhibition "Nomads: Masters of the Eurasian Steppe" are available through the University of Southern California's Center for Visual Anthropology, Los Angeles, CA 90089-0032. Edited by Professor Gary Seaman, each volume contains sixteen articles from American, Soviet, and Chinese authors. Volume 1 is Ecology and Empire: Nomads in the Cultural Evolution of the Old World; Volume 2 is Rulers from the Steppe: State Formation on the Eurasian periphery; Volume 3 is Evolution of Empire: Archaeological and Art Historical Studies of Eurasian Steppe Cultures. All three volumes are dedicated to the memory of Richard P. Feynman.

Appendix C

YOU are cordially invited to join the Friends of Tuva and receive a newsletter that lists various activities relating to Richard Feynman and Tuva. For information, please send a self-addressed, stamped envelope to:

Friends of Tuva
Box 70021
Pasadena, CA 91117
USA

Index

Abrams, Elliott, 197
Acheson, David, 156–57
Afghanistan, Soviet invasion of, 35, 42, 119
Alexandrov, Academician A. P., 143, 144, 145, 165, 169
Andropov, Yuri, 82, 88, 89, 93
arak, 91n
Aranchyn, Yuri, 192, 226, 227
Armenia, 118–20, 175, 223
Armenians, massacres of, 116n
asbestos, 28, 100
atomic weapons development, 7
Soviet, 22–23
Axel-Nilsson, Christian, 135, 146, 151, 152–54, 155, 156, 162, 163–64, 170, 173, 227
Axel-Nilsson, Hélène, 162
Azarpay, Guitty, 68
Azeris, 116n

Baku, 116–17
Bashkir ASSR, 185
Bashkir Curlies, 185, 186, 191

Basilov, Vladimir N., 135, 136, 137, 142, 143, 144, 146, 148–51, 159, 162, 164, 177, 181, 182, 186, 188, 190, 191, 194, 195–98, 204, 205, 206, 207, 208, 209, 212, 216, 225, 227
Begin, Menachem, 23
Bitburg, Germany, Reagan's visit to cemetery at, 115
Black, Craig, 168, 169, 172, 173, 206, 210
Boslough, John, 96–97
Braginsky, V. B., 54, 61
Bray, Faustin, 83
Brezhnev, Leonid, 33, 35, 81–82, 93, 108, 207
British Broadcasting Company (BBC), 159, 190, 208, 218n
Brown, J. Carter, 170–71, 173
Bush, George, 144n

California Institute of Technology (Caltech), 7, 52, 54, 64, 66, 72, 96

Cambodia, 23, 35
Campbell, Kurt M., 180
Camp David Accords, 23
Carruthers, Douglas, 21
Carter, Jimmy, 33, 35
Casetta, Mario, 62–63, 65, 74
Cavalry Maiden, The, 226n
Central Asia Newsletter, 34–35
Challenger disaster, 87, 88, 189
    investigation of, 7–8, 132, 144
    see also Rogers Commission
Charles, Prince of England, 55
Chernenko, Konstantin, 93, 107
Chernobyl, accident at, 169
China Pictorial, 45
Chinchig-ool (Chünchük-ool), 59
Chola, Mongush, 99–100
Christian Science Monitor, 22–23, 180,
    225
CIA, 89
clown diving, 23, 96, 173, 174
Cold War, 29
Cowan, Glen, 54–55, 57–58, 59–61,
    65, 67, 68, 69–70, 76, 77, 81–82,
    84–87, 88, 89, 92, 93, 97, 168,
    173, 174, 179, 181, 198, 227–28
    trip to Soviet Union with, 106–29
    trip to Sweden with, 130, 131, 132,
    133, 134–64, 166
Cowan, Tina, 54
Cycles of Superstition, 18–19, 181

Dalai Lama, 93
Daniloff, Nicholas, 172–73
Daryma, Ondar, 37, 39–41, 42, 43,
    44, 53, 57, 64–65, 67, 69–71, 76,
    81, 84, 92, 112, 173, 174, 175,
    183, 188, 215, 223, 224
Davis, Jeffrey, 173
Dead Poets Society, 67n
Dersu the Trapper, 47n

Dersu Uzala, 47, 85, 183, 186, 187,
    205
Diplomaragna feynmani, 229
Disneyland, 204, 208
drumming, 82, 104, 139–40
    by and with Feynman, 8, 16, 18–19,
    20, 23, 42, 65–66, 71–73, 181,
    193, 218, 223
Dugdale, G. S., 78–79
Durova, Nadezhda, 226n

Echmiadzin, 118–19
Eisenhower, Dwight D., 98, 115
Elias, Thomas S., 103, 104–6, 229
Encyclopaedia Britannica, 15, 206n
Esalen Institute, 82–84, 93, 94–95,
    97–98, 99, 144, 146, 151, 227
Etholén, Arvid Adolf, 177
Ewing, Thomas E., 35
Experiment for International Living,
    130

Falklands war, 76
FBI, 41, 76, 216
Feynman, Arlene, 97–98
Feynman, Carl, 13, 14, 15, 45
Feynman, Gweneth, 13, 15, 16, 45,
    47, 176, 198, 199, 206, 207, 214,
    219, 227–28
Feynman, Michelle, 13, 45
Feynman, Richard
    as accomplished artist, 157
    death of, 219
    dressed as Ladkhi lama, 45–47
    drumming by, 8, 16, 18–19, 20, 23,
    42, 65–66, 71–73, 181, 193, 218,
    223
    at Esalen Institute, 82–84, 93,
    94–95, 97–98, 99
    health of, 23, 63–64, 71, 73, 176,

177, 180–82, 204, 214–15,
218–19
in Las Vegas, 76–77
at Leighton's wedding, 173–74
Rogers Commission and, 7–8, 132,
144, 155, 156–57, 169–70, 179n
on Soviet government and Soviet
scientists, 141, 207–8
"Star Wars" project and, 179n
summary of life of, 7–8
travels of, 16
and Tuva project, 14–17 (*see also*
Tannu Tuva)
Feynman Lectures on Physics, The, 8,
123, 128, 140
Freedom of Information Act, 41n
Friends of Tuva, 62, 87, 92, 99, 131,
144, 171, 223n
inadvertent founding of, 56
invitation to join, 56n
memorial plaque planned by, 229
Silverlake chapter of, 74

Gell-Mann, Murray, 66
Geo, 42, 90, 91
J. Paul Getty Museum, 211–12
Ginzburg, V. L., 54, 61
Gorbachev, Mikhail, 107, 112, 113,
114–15, 131, 146, 170, 176, 179,
184, 197
Göteborg Historical Museum, 130,
133, 134–35, 152–54, 155, 164
Great Soviet Encyclopedia, 19, 28
Grishin, V. V., 92–93, 107–8
Gromyko, Andrei, 138
Grosvenor, Gilbert M., 96, 99

Hakim, Albert, 197
Hall, Fawn, 197
Halley's comet, 168

Harmonic Choir, 67, 74, 217
harmonic choirs (overtone choirs),
67n
Harner, Michael, 227
Harris, Julie, 81
Helsinki, 108
höömei, 41
see also throat singing
Humphrey, Caroline M., 48–49, 225
Hykes, David, 67, 217

Idiosyncratic thinking, seminar on,
83–84, 93–94, 97
Institute of Ethnography in Moscow,
61, 65, 85, 124, 125, 126, 149–50
International Research and Exchange
(IREX), 87, 89
Intourist, 32, 33, 53, 59, 110, 112,
113, 114, 115, 116
Inuit women, 36
Iran, 23, 35, 42
Iran-Contra scandal, 184, 197, 203
Ivory Merchant, The, 19, 20, 66

Jefferson, Thomas, 141
John Paul I, Pope, 23
Johnson, Samuel, 20
John Wayne Cancer Clinic, 8n, 63,
218n
Jonson, Elizabeth, 137, 138, 141–42
Jonson, Emma, 134, 135, 137
Jonson, Mats, 133, 134, 135, 137–42,
146, 148, 154, 164

Kadafi, Moammar, 23
Kapitsa, A. P., 143, 169, 170, 171,
172, 177, 181, 184, 186, 190,
191, 204, 205–9, 211, 212, 214,
216, 217, 219, 221

Kapitsa, Eugenia, 209, 211, 217
Kapitsa, Pyotr, 205–6
Kapitsa, Sergei, 208
Karapachinsky, Yuri, 103
Kasparov, Gary, 117
Kazakhs: Horsemen of China, 194n
Kazarian, Eduard, 119
Keller, Peter, 166–67, 171, 173, 176,
    177–78, 182, 190, 191, 192, 194,
    196, 198, 200, 204, 205, 206,
    208, 209, 215, 216
Kennedy, Edward, 144, 146
KGB, 41n, 82, 112, 128, 172, 207
Khmer Rouge regime, 23
Khomeini, Ayatollah, 23
Khrushchev, Nikita, 82, 108, 109,
    123, 172
Kineer, Jack, 65–66
Kirghiz, 112
Korea, 174–76, 223
Korean Airlines flight 007, downing
    of, 88–89, 171
Krueger, John R., 36, 44, 64, 67–68,
    75–76, 134, 229
Kryukov, M. V., 143n
kumiss, 142
Kurosawa, Akira, 47, 85, 183
Kurylov, Vadim, 138, 142, 148–51,
    164
Kwan, Phoebe, 69, 154, 155, 168,
    173–77, 178, 185, 193, 198, 206,
    211, 214, 216, 221–25, 228
Kyrgys, Marx, 128
Kyrgys, Zoya Kyrgysovna, 217

Ladakh, 45–47
Lake Tere-Khol, 102–3, 129, 138
Lalanne, Jack, 111n
Lamin, Vladimir, 138, 148–51, 164,
    176–77, 178, 182–83, 192, 193,
    204, 216, 221–22, 227

"Last Journey of a Genius," 218n
Las Vegas, 76–77
Lattimore, Owen, 34, 193, 194, 195,
    201, 204, 209
Lebanon, Israeli invasion of, 76
Leighton, Alan, 14, 20, 26, 28, 29,
    69n, 78, 87, 130, 132, 133, 134,
    141–42, 164, 173
Leighton, Linda, 130, 134, 141–42,
    164, 173, 229
Lenin, V. I., 33, 108, 109, 110, 112,
    116
Leningrad, 110–11
Lennon, John, 42
Leonov, Nikolai I., 78n
Leptons and Quarks, 122
Levin, Ted, 67, 217–18, 222n, 229
Libya, 23, 168
Life magazine, 98, 108
Li Youyi, 211
London, Jack, 208
Los Angeles County Museum of Art,
    166
loyalty oaths, 29
Lubyanka Prison, 112, 172
Luehrsen, Thomas, 197–98, 214

McAuliffe, Christa, 132
MacNeil/Lehrer Newshour, 188
MAD magazine, 127
Maenchen, Anna, 68–69
Mänchen-Helfen, Otto, 24–26, 27, 34,
    35, 49, 58, 68, 77, 78, 136, 175
Manhattan Project, 7
Marneus, Shirley, 65
Marshall, Sylvan, 169, 171, 173, 177,
    200
massage, 94–95
Melodii Tuvy, 61, 64, 66, 74
Mifune, Toshiro, 47
Mir publishers, 122–23, 146

Mondale, Walter, 99
Moore, Marianne, 108
Morton, Donald, 63, 97, 176
Moscow International Film Festival,
    203
Munger, Ned, 66
Munzuk, Maxim, 183–84, 186–87,
    204–5, 223
Murphey, Michael, 144, 229
Murray, David, 103, 104–5
music, see throat singing
Mystery of Lake Tere-Khol, The, 102

NASA, 8
National Gallery of Art, 170
National Geographic, 42, 45, 96–97, 99,
    106, 218
Natural History Museum of Los
    Angeles County, 166–67, 168,
    169, 170, 178n, 180, 181, 192,
    194, 205, 206, 225
Neher, Sara and H. Victor, 98, 99
Newton, Wayne, 125
New Yorker magazine, 170, 173
Nixon, Richard, 105, 222
"Nomads of Eurasia" exhibition, 143,
    182, 194, 224, 225–26, 228
    arrangements concerning, 204–13,
    215–16
    see also "On the Silk Road"
    exhibition
Nomads of South Siberia, 47–53, 139
W. W. Norton, 169, 170
"Nova," 155
Novodevichi cemetary, 108, 109, 123
Nureyev, Rudolf, 185

O'Connor, Sandra Day, 55
Ohnuki, Masako, 183
Ohnuki, Tohru, 8n, 85

Ohnuki, Yasushi, 85, 183
Okun, Lev, 122
Olson, James, 166, 167, 177, 182, 190,
    192, 194, 198, 200
Olympic Games, 35, 42, 95–96
"On the Silk Road" exhibition, 126,
    129, 130–31, 132, 137, 141, 143,
    145–46, 172, 221–22
    see also "Nomads of Eurasia"
    exhibition
Orgu, K. X., 40
Orkhon-Yenisei inscriptions, 55
overtone choirs (harmonic choirs), 67n

Pacific Asia Museum, 166
Palme, Olaf, 166
Palmer, Arnold, 97
Park Chung Hee, assassination of, 35
Personal Observations on the Reliability of
    the Shuttle, 179n
"Pleasure of Finding Things Out,
    The," 155, 218n
Politburo of the CPSU, 89, 92
Pol Pot, 35
Posner, Sylvia, 47n
postage stamps, 14, 20–21, 24, 25,
    40–41, 63
Pravda, 84–85
Princeton University, 7
Proctor, Dr., 229
Promptov, Yuri, 77n, 80
pyrophillite, 101n

QED: The Strange Theory of Light and
    Matter, 83n, 122
"Quest for Tannu Tuva, The," 218n

Radio Kyzyl, 30, 32
Radio Moscow, 24, 27–29, 32, 42, 53

Reagan, Ronald, 42, 43, 55, 81, 93,
    99, 114–15, 131–32, 146, 168,
    170, 176, 179, 203, 227
Regan, Donald, 179
Reise ins asiatische Tuwa, 24–26, 27,
    58, 69n, 78
Republic of China: A Reference Book, 56
restaurants, Soviet, 121–22
Ride, Sally, 88
Road to Oblivion, 19–20, 47n
Rogers, William P., 179n
Rogers Commission, 7–8, 132, 144,
    155, 156–57, 169–70, 179n
Romanov, Grigoriy, 107
Royal Geographical Society, 78
Russians, The, 108
Rust, Matthias, 197
Rutishauser, Thomas, 8, 139

Sadat, Anwar, 23
Safecracker Suite, 8n
safecracking, 7
Sakharov, Andrei, 35, 141, 184, 207
SALT II Treaty, 33
Scythian bronze plaque, 55, 226, 228
Scythian gold sculpture, 24, 27, 136,
    137
SDI ("Star Wars" project), 179, 180
Seaman, Gary, 204, 209
Secord, Richard, 195
Sedip-ool (Tanov), 59
shamanism, 151, 227
    Tuvan, 28, 48, 51, 52, 138–40, 223
Sharif, Omar, 226
Shear, William A., 229
Shephard's Tale, A, 57–58
Sherlock, Karen, 217, 218
Shetler, Stanwyn, 103, 104, 229
Shevardnadze, Eduard, 117, 179
Shirshin, Grigori, 100
Shonchur, 139–40

Shultz, George, 88, 179
Silow, Axel, 135, 138
Silversides, Brock, 81
Singer, André, 194–95, 197, 201,
    209
Smith, Hedrick, 108
Smith, Samantha, 88, 89, 92, 222
Smithsonian Institution, 135, 177,
    216, 228
Sochi, 120–22
Solidarity, 81
Songs of Tuva, 217
South Pacific, 65, 71–73
Soviet Academy of Sciences, 34, 126,
    144, 146, 152, 154, 159, 168,
    182, 193, 195, 204, 205, 206,
    207, 213, 214, 216, 219, 221, 224
Soviet Life magazine, 98, 99–103, 129,
    226
Soviet Union, 106–29
    see also Tannu Tuva
Sovinfilm, 186, 188, 190, 191, 193,
    195–202, 203, 204, 207
Stalin, Joseph, 106, 108, 116, 117
"Star Wars" project, 179, 180
Stepanova, Eugenia, 32
stirrups, 143
stone carvings, Tuvan, 55, 101–2, 125,
    224
Strahlenberg, Philip Johan von, 163
Surely You're Joking, Mr. Feynman!, 7n,
    97, 109, 122, 123, 128
Surikov, Alexander, 186, 188, 190,
    196, 198, 200, 202, 204, 205
Sweden, 130–66
Sykes, Christopher, 155, 157, 159,
    165, 178, 189, 190, 194, 198,
    217, 218

Tahitian drumming, 65–66
Taiwan, 56–57

Tannu Tuva
    art of, 24, 55, 125, 136–37, 226,
        228, back jacket
    correspondence with Ondar Daryma
        of, 31–41, 42, 43, 44, 53, 64–65,
        81, 173, 174, 175, 188, 215
    exhibition and film projects as
        attempts to reach, 130–219
    formal and informal research
        concerning, 19–71, 74–129
    origin of Feynman-Leighton project
        concerning, 14–17
    photo of Feynman, Cowan, and
        Leighton in newspaper of, 85–87,
        89
    postage stamps as introduction to,
        14, 20–21, 24, 25, 40–41, 63
    shamans in, 28, 48, 51, 52, 138–40,
        223
    summary of recent events
        concerning, 221–29
    throat singing of, 36, 41, 62–63,
        66–67, 76, 100, 105, 217, 223,
        229
    trip by Kwan and Leighton to,
        221–25
Tapit (Dapyt), Oyun S., 59
TASS, 42, 95
Tbilisi, 117–18
Thatcher, Margaret, 29
"This Week with David Brinkley,"
    184
Thorne, Kip, 61
Three Mile Island accident, 29
throat singing, 36, 41, 62–63, 66–67,
    76, 100, 105, 197, 217, 223,
    229
Time magazine, 114, 225
TNIIYaLI (Tuvan Scientific Research
    Institute of Language, Literature,
    and History), 32, 37, 60, 70–71,
    224, 226, 229

Toka, Salchak, 57–59
Tolstoy, Leo, 138
Tournament of Roses Parade, 185–86,
    191, 229
Tuva, see Tannu Tuva
Tuvan Manual, 36, 37, 40, 44, 186,
    229
Tuva Trivia game, 183
Tuva: Voices from the Center of Asia,
    217n
Tuvinskaya Pravda, 84–85, 87, 89, 90,
    95, 141, 145
Tyva Tooldar, 40, 43, 53

Uchenye Zapiski, 57
U. S. News & World Report, 172
Unknown Mongolia, 21
uranium, 22–23
USSR, 106–29
    see also Tannu Tuva
USSR Academy of Sciences, see
    Soviet Academy of Sciences

VAAP, 157, 169, 170, 176
Vainshtein, Sevyan, 47–54, 55, 57, 61,
    65, 76, 81, 84, 85, 87, 89, 102–3,
    109, 112, 122, 124–29, 131, 132,
    135–46, 148–51, 155–64, 169,
    176, 180, 181, 184, 186, 188,
    217, 221, 226
Van Pelt, Erica and Harold, 206
Velikhov, E. P., 219, 221
Vietnam, 35
Vitale, Tom, 66–67
Volgograd, 112–15

What Do You Care What Other People
    Think?, 98n, 179n
Whitaker's Almanac, 79–80

whortleberries, 101, 106
Wojtyla, Karol Cardinal, 23

Yeltsin, Boris, 108, 144n
Yosemite National Park, 208, 214, 216
Young Pioneers, 88, 117, 222

Zagrevskaya, Yelena, 188
Zakarov, Gennadi, 173
Zenzinov, Vladimir, 19–20, 47n
Zirin, Mary Fleming, 22, 30, 47, 62, 67, 226
Zorthian, Jirayr, 212

RICHARD FEYNMAN (1918–1988) is portrayed here by Pasadena artist Sylvia Posner in the garb of a Ladakhi monk. (The costume, based on photographs in the *National Geographic*, was made by his wife, Gweneth, for a costume party. Had the geographical restrictions allowed it, he would have dressed as a lama from Tannu Tuva.)

In the background is the landscape of Los Alamos, where Feynman worked on the Manhattan Project during the Second World War. The opened padlock has both literal and symbolic significance. In his right hand is a "Feynman diagram," which Feynman originally invented as a kind of shorthand to help him remember where he was in a complex calculation. Such diagrams have helped physicists around the world unlock the mysteries of nature. (The diagram here shows one possible way that two electrons can go through space and time: one electron emits a photon—represented by the wavy line—and the other electron absorbs it.)

A full-color poster measuring 21½ by 29½ inches is available for $15 (one poster), $28 (two posters), or $40 (three posters) postpaid. Please send a check to:

Ralph Leighton
Box 70021
Pasadena, CA 91117
USA

All proceeds go to the John Wayne Cancer Clinic at UCLA, whose doctors gave Feynman an additional six years of life—and gave the rest of us an additional six years of Richard Feynman.